DATE DUE

THE REFERENCE SHELF   VOLUME 44 NUMBER 5

CHINA

NEW FORCE IN WORLD AFFAIRS

EDITED BY
IRWIN ISENBERG

THE H. W. WILSON COMPANY
NEW YORK   1972

THE REFERENCE SHELF

The books in this series contain reprints of articles, excerpts from books, and addresses on current issues and social trends in the United States and other countries. There are six separately bound numbers in each volume, all of which are generally published in the same calendar year. One number is a collection of recent speeches; each of the others is devoted to a single subject and gives background information and discussion from various points of view, concluding with a comprehensive bibliography. Books in the series may be purchased individually or on subscription.

Library of Congress Cataloging in Publication Data

Isenberg, Irwin, comp.
  China: new force in world affairs.

  (The Reference shelf, v. 44, no. 5)
  SUMMARY: A compilation of articles presenting
various points of view on contemporary life and govern-
ment policy in mainland China.
  Bibliography: p.
  1. China (People's Republic of China, 1949-   ).
[1. China (People's Republic of China, 1949-   )]
I. Title. II. Series.
DS777.55.I73   327.51   72-8953
ISBN 0-8242-0468-9

PREFACE

For some twenty years, the Communist regime of mainland China was isolated from much of the world community. Though containing one quarter of mankind, Communist China had only limited diplomatic, economic, or cultural relations with other nations. It was also at odds with the Soviet Union, which in the 1950s had been China's close ally.

For two decades the United States had led the campaign to contain and quarantine China and had successfully lobbied to keep the world's most populous country out of the United Nations. The United States gave no diplomatic recognition to the Communist regime and instead recognized the Nationalist regime of Chiang Kai-shek which had fled to the offshore island of Taiwan after being defeated by Communist forces on the mainland in 1949. During this two-decade period, an army under the United Nations flag and comprising chiefly US troops had fought the Chinese after their intervention in the Korean conflict in the early 1950s. Throughout these years, the United States supplied a protective military shield over its Taiwan ally against a possible attack from the mainland.

Meanwhile, mainland China was making a mighty effort to speed its economic development and mounted a campaign to win friends among the less-developed nations of Asia and Africa. Through a combination of force, determination, ideological commitment, skill, and the labor of its citizens, the regime has recorded significant economic gains in some fields, though China is still a poor country. Nevertheless, the pattern of stagnation and torpor that had characterized China in the decades and generations before the Communists seized power in 1949 has been altered. In the words of Chinese leader Mao Tse-tung, China has stood up.

By the beginning of the 1970s, a majority of nations recognized that the continued exclusion of China from the world community was no longer a viable policy. Some, such as Great Britain, Canada, and France, as well as a number of nations in Asia and Africa, had already opened diplomatic and trading relations with China. Others saw little to be gained from excluding China from the United Nations.

The United States Government, too, endorsed the need for change in its China policy. Thus, in 1971, it voted along with a majority of United Nations members to accept China in the world organization. At the same time, however, Taiwan was expelled from the United Nations. This was a serious setback for the United States, which had hoped to legitimize a two-China policy, allowing both the mainland and Taiwan to occupy United Nations seats.

In February 1972, President Nixon went to Peking, the Chinese capital, to try to normalize relations between the United States and China. Although some Americans opposed this move, the President's initiative was generally applauded in the United States, as well as by our allies and by the so-called third world of less-developed countries.

In the United States it was hoped that the President's talks in Peking and the resulting increased contacts between US and Chinese officials might hasten the end of the Vietnam war. Any improvement in US-Chinese relations also was significant in terms of future trade with the mainland, not only by the United States but by such countries as Japan and the industrialized nations of Western Europe. No less important was the effect any US-Chinese rapprochement might have on the simmering and dangerous Sino-Soviet border conflicts.

All these factors have resulted in a need for more information about China. Yet to compile even a brief book on China is an intimidating task and a major challenge. The subject is vast, complex, and relatively unknown—even though a number of journalists and other visitors have been allowed to tour the mainland in the past several years.

In order to present as complete a picture of contemporary China as possible, this book has been divided into four sections covering salient aspects of life and government policy on the mainland. The first section describes some of the major characteristics of Chinese society. It should be noted that these characteristics have their roots in thousands of years of history and so form a link between the traditional past and the revolutionary present.

The second section deals with what is known as the Cultural Revolution, one of the most startling and disruptive events in the history of the Communist regime. The Cultural Revolution plunged China into chaos, but it also gave a view of the kind of society and individual Mao and his supporters hoped to create.

The third section surveys the social and economic scene. A special note of caution must be sounded, however. Although this section contains eyewitness accounts, it should be remembered that visitors to China can travel only to selected government-chosen places. Moreover, figures relating to the economy are scattered and often unreliable, thus making analysis difficult.

The last section discusses foreign policy issues. Particular attention is focused on the Sino-Soviet dispute and on Chinese diplomacy in Africa. This section also reviews policy issues facing the United States with regard to mainland China.

The author wishes to thank the editors and publishers who have granted permission to reprint the extracts in this book. He also wishes to thank his colleague Prem Pathak and Errol Isenberg for their editorial assistance.

IRWIN ISENBERG

September 1972

A NOTE TO THE READER

For background material on the Sino-Soviet conflict, the reader should consult the editor's earlier compilation *The Russian-Chinese Rift* (The Reference Shelf, Volume 38, Number 2), published in 1966.

CONTENTS

PREFACE 3

MAP: COMMUNIST CHINA 10

I. CHINESE SOCIETY AND BELIEFS

Editor's Introduction 11
Michel Oksenberg. China's Five Belief Systems 12
What It Means to Be Chinese .... Newsweek 26
Coming of Age in Communist China ...... Newsweek 32
Lisa Hobbs. How the Oldest Civilization in the World
    Brings Up Its Youngest Members ....
    .... Parents Magazine & Better Family Living 38

II. THE CULTURAL REVOLUTION

Editor's Introduction 48
As Red China Plunges Deeper Into Chaos ....
    .... U.S. News & World Report 49
Decision of the Chinese Communist Party Central Com-
    mittee Concerning the Great Cultural Revolution
    .... Survey of the China Mainland Press 55

The Cultural Revolution: Its Zigs and Zags 67

Theodore Hsi-en Chen. A Nation in Agony ....
.... Problems of Communism 71

III. HOW THE CHINESE LIVE AND WORK

Editor's Introduction 83

Robert P. Martin. China Revisited ....
.... U.S. News & World Report 84

Life in the Middle Kingdom .... Time 96

Robert Keatley. Making Do ...... Wall Street Journal 103

Roland Berger. "Beckoning a New Generation" ......
.... Nation 111

Gael Alderson-Smith. Toil on the Farms ....
.... Washington Post 118

IV. CHINA AND THE WORLD

Editor's Introduction 124

Our China Policy 126

Text of Communiqué .... New York Times 142

George T. Yu. Peking's African Diplomacy ....
.... Problems of Communism 148

Stefan T. Possony. The Permanence of Conflict ......
.... Modern Age 165

William Beecher. Shift in Strategy by Peking Is Seen
.... New York Times 186

Franklin W. Houn. Chinese Foreign Policy in Perspective .... Bulletin of the Atomic Scientists 190

BIBLIOGRAPHY 207

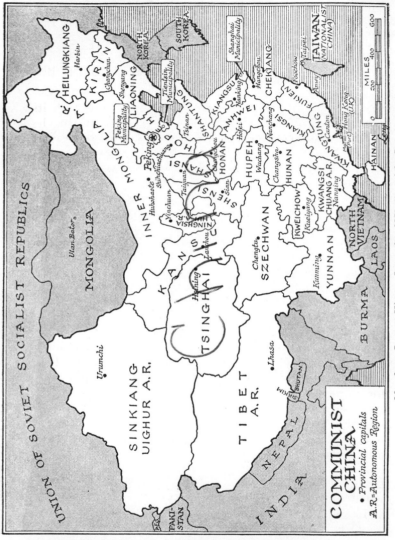

Map from *Current History*, September 1970. Copyright ©
1970 by Current History, Inc. Reprinted by permission.

I. CHINESE SOCIETY AND BELIEFS

EDITOR'S INTRODUCTION

China has an old and traditional culture, one with its roots planted firmly in millennia of history even as it struggles to build a new way of life and a new society under the leadership of the Communist regime. These old roots, embodied in an interrelated and complex system of customs and beliefs, concern personal conduct and ethics, family relationships, the place of the individual in his family and his village, the duties imposed upon him by his place in society, and his attitudes toward those in authority.

To the extent that this traditional value system is able to integrate itself with the goals and aspirations of the Communist leadership there is a continuity in Chinese history between the past and the pattern of contemporary life. But where the old values act as a barrier to present goals as enunciated by the government, there is necessarily tension and disruption.

This section surveys some of the major characteristics of Chinese society, as perceived by Western observers. In a sense, the articles in this section form part of the foundation for an understanding of China and the Chinese. For example, the closely reasoned first article by a student of Chinese affairs identifies five "belief systems" which compete for supporters in China today. These five systems, all of which can be traced through various aspects of Chinese history, are the traditional, revolutionary, bureaucratic, technological, and totalitarian elements. By understanding how each of these belief systems operates in the Chinese context, the reader can gain an insight into national behavior and motives.

The next two articles are taken from *Newsweek*. The articles appeared just prior to President Nixon's 1972 trip to

China and were an attempt to introduce the American reader
to an unknown—the Chinese man. The first *Newsweek* article
concentrates on the images the Chinese people have sketched
about themselves and the world around them and reveals
much about family life as well. The second describes the
value system as transmitted to children, teenagers, and adults.
As convincing portraits of an Asian society, these articles
have much to offer the American reader.

The last article in this section is an account of child
rearing, education, and family life which draws a vivid picture of the society today. Of particular interest in this and
the previous articles is the depiction of the striking differences
between American and Chinese modes of living and social
patterns.

CHINA'S FIVE BELIEF SYSTEMS [1]

Five "pure" belief systems compete for adherents in contemporary China. For the sake of simplicity, these can be
labeled traditional, revolutionary, bureaucratic, technological and totalitarian systems. To be sure, these beliefs do not
exist in the material world; they only reside in the minds of
the Chinese people. Moreover, few Chinese have a single,
systematic ideology; rather, most Chinese, the top leaders included, have various, often conflicting, beliefs. In a sense,
therefore, the five coherent sets of beliefs described below
are analytical constructs illuminating a complex situation
but having no "objective" existence.

The Traditional System

The traditional culture incorporated many diverse philosophies. Indeed, as wide a spectrum of beliefs existed in the
Chinese as in the Western tradition. Hence, when we speak
of traditional beliefs, we do not refer solely to Confucianism,

[1] From *China: The Convulsive Society*, pamphlet by Michel Oksenberg, assistant professor of political science, Columbia University. (Headline Series no
203) Foreign Policy Association. 345 E. 46th St. New York 10017. '70. p 5-19.
Reprinted by permission from Headline Series no 203. Copyright 1970 by the
Foreign Policy Association, Inc.

Taoism or Buddhism, but rather to a widely held amalgam of many philosophies.

Pivotal concepts in this traditional philosophy are: the premium placed upon an ordered, hierarchical society; the value attached to harmony, loyalty and propriety; the belief that man should live in harmony with nature; and the central role assigned to family. According to the traditional credo, man achieves spiritual fulfillment through social action. But his proper social role is severely circumscribed. Man should not remold his society, but rather should play the roles expected of him. Each person is born into a net of obligations which he must honor. A person who properly meets his obligations, in theory, obtains great satisfaction and moreover secures the obligations of others. When enough people in society abide by the roles assigned them, then the society will be peaceful and well regulated. Through personal example and discipline of the realm, the national leader is responsible for insuring that his people know virtue and act upon it.

Several aspects of this tradition stand out. Overt conflict is considered unpleasant and avoidable. Knowing how and when to yield to preserve a facade of harmony is a valued art. Interdependence is encouraged; independence, discouraged. Excellence in interpersonal relations earns praise; boldness wins scorn. Conformity, not initiative, is prized. Men aspire to be social engineers, not to explore the earth. Ideally, the educational system yields cultured generalists, not technical specialists.

The essence of the traditional system, fostering social stability and continuity, was recorded in an interview with a poor Chinese servant woman:

> The generations stretch back thousands of years to the great ancestor parents. They stretch for thousands of years into the future, generation upon generation. Seen in proportion to this great array, the individual is but a small thing. But on the other hand, no individual can drop out. Each is a link in the great

ᣛ   chain. No one can drop out without breaking the
     chain. A woman stands with one hand grasping the
     generations that have gone before and with the other,
     generations to come.

Such notions made old China a society built for the ages.
Each family generation subordinated itself to the memory
of its ancestors and identified with the welfare of its descendants. Rather than demanding immediate gratification, efforts seemed rewarded if they promised a better position for
the family line. These are values tied to an impoverished,
relatively stagnant economic system. People did not expect
annual improvement in their welfare; they only hoped that
in time their family might obtain a larger piece of the existing pie.

The coming of the West in the 1800s challenged these
beliefs. Indeed, by the May Fourth movement of 1919
[a student-led nationalistic campaign], few Chinese intellectuals believed that traditional values were relevant to
China's new situation. But, for several reasons, the deeply
ingrained beliefs and customs did not disappear. While intellectuals and some businessmen may have searched abroad
for values that seemed more suitable, millions of Chinese in
the hinterlands could only draw inspiration from native
ideas. In addition, these values were still congruent with the
interests of certain sectors of society, particularly the upper
classes in rural areas and the elderly. Moreover, while many
Chinese rejected their traditions on the conscious level, they
retained them unconsciously. Psychologically, it has proven
difficult for many Chinese to reject their proud heritage;
rather, they have attempted to salvage portions of their tradition while convincing themselves that much which they
accept from the West already existed in China anyway. Finally, traditional Chinese values persist because the factors
which gave rise to them persist: certain distinctive childhood
rearing practices, poverty and a densely populated agrarian
society vulnerable to the vagaries of nature. For all of these

reasons, the traditional belief system remains a vital force in present-day China, particularly in the countryside.

Although no major political figure openly advocates the traditional belief system in China today, its continuing influence is revealed in concrete practices. For example, the pivotal role of Mao is, in many ways, similar to that of the emperors of old. As with previous rulers, supposedly he embodies virtue, and his example and discipline order the realm. Deified, his picture appears in peasant homes where idols previously were kept, and peasants officially are urged to bow before his likeness while orally pledging their loyalty to him. But tradition is seen less in officially sanctioned policy than in the persistence of old customs, especially in more remote rural areas: extended families, arranged marriages and traditional commercial practices.

Revolutionary Beliefs

A revolutionary strand of thought has long coexisted with the dominant traditional strand. It came to the fore during China's periodic peasant revolts and in the early twentieth century was reinforced by the importation of populist and anarchist beliefs from the West and Japan. Mao has added to its vitality by eloquently articulating, publicizing and acting upon much of this doctrine.

The revolutionary credo supports an egalitarian redistribution of wealth and opportunity. It places great confidence in man's ability, through sheer will and energy, to remold his society; it considers the Chinese masses, particularly the peasants, to be the motive force of history and dismisses the necessity of having an elite to lead society. It emphasizes the need for a spiritual transformation of mankind, not a technical transformation of man's environment. It considers the root evil on earth to be exploitation of man by other men and traces such other evils as poverty and illness to it. It attacks those segments of society which it deems exploitative, particularly merchants, bureaucrats, intellectuals and urban dwellers. It calls for society to be restructured and, more importantly, for man to transform his desires, so that he no longer would seek to profit at another's expense.

How to change man's attitudes thus becomes a central concern of the revolutionary doctrine. In essence, this ideology distrusts organization and champions spontaneity. The rationale behind this particular aspect of the belief system deserves explanation. The discipline and control of organizations often prevent liberating experiences. Participation in spontaneous collective movements, on the other hand, supposedly severs a person's ties to his past, enabling him to achieve a sense of community with his contemporaries. Losing his old individual identity, he partakes of the greater spirit of the group and thereby achieves a spiritual transformation. Mao calls this submergence of the individual to the group, "Putting public ahead of self." ...

The utopia which this doctrine envisions is therefore a classless society, for only in such a society will exploitation cease. As soon as classes emerge, some profit at the expense of others. Hence, specialization and narrow professional loyalties are undesirable. The psychic barriers between farmers, industrial workers and intellectuals must be removed, and differences between urban and rural areas kept at a minimum. When uniformity is achieved—when everybody is more or less the same—loneliness and exploitation will be eliminated and true community attained.

One other aspect of the revolutionary ideology in China should be made explicit: its provincialism. It rejects the relevance of the outside world to China's current needs. It emphasizes the innate capacity of the Chinese people to transform their own society while denigrating the value or necessity of foreign assistance. Accordingly, a watchword of current Chinese foreign policy is *tzu-li keng-sheng,* meaning "self reliance" or, more precisely, "regeneration through our own efforts."

Further, the revolutionary vision of the good society is applied globally. Ideally, the nations of the world should be united through shared values, not through interdependence.

Peace can come to the world only when nations are culturally, economically and militarily independent, and therefore can deal with each other as equals. Hence, the revolutionary doctrine predisposes its Chinese adherents to turn inward, to shun trade and aid, cultural exchanges or entangling military alliances, and to pride themselves on self-sufficiency.

Revolutionary beliefs are reflected in many specific policies in China. Bureaucrats periodically must engage in hard labor to break down the barriers between "mental" and "physical" work. Small rural industries are developed to eliminate differences between urban and rural areas. The Chinese military apparatus does not have a formal ranking system. Attempts are made constantly to reduce wage differentials. The regime judges people as much on their attitudes as on their competence. The educational system and the propaganda apparatus aim more at changing attitudes than at teaching proficiency. These policies clearly give China a radical, experimental air.

Mao, as previously noted, certainly embraces these revolutionary ideas and programs, but not as completely as some of his supporters. Above all, it must be remembered, Mao is a dialectician. His quest is for synthesis. He is attempting to build a society which will truly reconcile many contradictory but equally desirable elements: discipline and freedom with unity of will and individuality. Hence, intellectually, Mao embraces both revolutionary beliefs and their opposites. Believing in the dialectic, Mao prefers not to choose one ethic over another, but rather to search for a synthesis. But emotionally, Mao is predisposed toward revolutionary values.

What remain to be explained are the reasons for the strength of revolutionary beliefs. Their support by Mao obviously is a crucial factor. Yet, since these beliefs were powerful in China before Mao, reference simply to Mao is insufficient. Rather, we must ask: Why do revolutionary beliefs elicit such support? A crucial consideration is that populist, egalitarian and antibureaucratic impulses seem to elicit a response from the rural poor. Indeed, around the world, peasants appear to have dual tendencies—usually conservative but also capable of conversion to violent, short-lived, radical movements. And in China upon occasion, peasants enthusiastically have responded to calls to remake their harsh world—for example, the T'ai-p'ing Rebellion of the 1850s and the Boxer Rebellion of the 1890s. The Chinese Communists, after all, came to power through peasant support, and a significant portion of Chinese officials just below the top echelons were recruited into the Chinese Communist party (CCP) as illiterate, impoverished peasant youths. Is it any wonder, then, that some of the values of the social classes which brought about the sweeping upheaval in China would continue to have such force only twenty years after the revolution?

But the revolutionary ideology has strength for another reason. The industrialization process generates its own opposition. Indeed, the consequences of industrialization spread unevenly through society, with many people feeling its harmful effects before enjoying its benefits. . . .

The Technological Ethic

The technological ethic advocates man's triumph over nature. Man, through science, can control and transform his material environment and, thereby, eliminate poverty and disease. Further, according to this optimistic assessment of man's ability to dominate the earth, technological change provides man with the capacity, indeed the need, to initiate social and political change. The technological ethic, therefore, generates policies which hasten scientific development, industrialization and production; it encourages skepticism, bold experimentation and individual initiative and achievement. Competition and conflict, which stimulate research and social change, are preferred to the stifling effect of harmony and compromise. The ethic judges men more on their technical competence and accomplishments than on their personality, morality or background. Rather than encouraging man to fulfill social obligations, it calls upon him to realize his full potential through the manipulation of material things.

Man's crowning achievement, the place where he has built an environment in which he is free to give full reign to his intellectual creativity, is the city. Even the choice of words reflects the preference for the city: *urbane* and *cosmopolitan* are equated with culture; and *bucolic* or *rustic* are often equated with coarseness.

When the technological ethic holds sway, people expect and strive for swift economic improvements, and the society becomes expansive and innovative. The technological ethic also encourages an empirical approach to problems. Choices tend to be made on narrow, technical grounds, and the raising of more profound, time-consuming ideological considerations tends to be discouraged. Arguments supported by production, wage and budget data tend to be more persuasive than metaphysical or moralistic arguments.

The belief in technology is relatively recent in China; it is primarily the result of the Western impact. The technological ethic won converts initially because military power demonstrably accrued to those states accepting it. Gradually, moreover, people whose interests often coincide with the technological ethic—scientists, engineers, factory managers, professional military officers, to an extent skilled industrial workers, and so on—began to acquire influence in China. In addition, it seems that the industrial ethic has its exponents among the top leadership. Premier Chou En-lai seems in many ways to be its most articulate spokesman, but other leaders, particularly those in charge of the nation's economy, have defended technical values against attacks from the supporters of the other value systems.

Certainly, the signs are plentiful that China as a nation— Mao included—is committed to the transformation of China into an industrial power in the world. Thus, China is pushing its development of nuclear weapons and modern delivery systems. In the past twenty years many large industrial centers have sprung up in the interior: Paotow, Chengchow,

Lanchow, Taiyuan, Chengtu. Top-flight scientists are partially shielded from political turmoil. The land is scoured for its natural resources, which are abundant. The number of engineering and technical personnel has been soaring: 164,000 in 1952; 449,000 in 1956; approximately 1.1 million in 1960; and well over 1.5 million in 1964. The social and material basis to support a technological ethic is gaining in China, but in a basically agrarian society of 750 million people, without an indigenous belief system on which it can be grafted, this ethic has not yet become dominant.

Bureaucratic Ethic

The bureaucratic ethic, unlike traditional or revolutionary beliefs, does not encompass a total view of the ideal society. Rather, recognizing that the means affect ends, it focuses more upon the necessary mechanisms and procedures for maintaining and developing society. The bureaucratic ideology emphasizes that man's welfare depends upon his ability to undertake complex tasks. This in turn requires subdividing the tasks into manageable work assignments, distributing the tasks among individuals and developing ongoing institutions to coordinate the effort. Institutions demand from their members subordination, routine and specialization.

The bureaucratic ethic, then, encourages virtues which facilitate effective organization: loyalty, collegiality, obedience and efficiency. In addition, life within the organization becomes an important source of personal satisfaction. As a result, concern with rewards distributed within the organization—salary, rank and so on—and with the prestige and power of one's organization in society are inextricably part of the ethic. This set of beliefs leads its adherents to develop elaborate doctrine about the pivotal aspects of bureaucracy: recruitment, indoctrination into the norms of the organization, promotion and discipline.

Ideally, the bureaucratic ethic fosters rule through written law. These laws define the tasks of bureaucratic positions and require others to obey the edicts originating from these designated positions, regardless of which individual holds the position. That is, power resides in institutions, not men. At its best, the bureaucratic vision protects citizens from the arbitrary exercise of power. A politically neutral civil service dutifully administers legal codes which reflect the popular will. But at its worst, the bureaucratic ethic leads to empire building, buck passing, blundering officials, rigid rules, inertia and venality.

The bureaucratic ethic, both good and bad, has long prospered in China. Even under the Communists, particularly in the mid-1950s, there was widespread advocacy of establishing a codified legal system, and significant steps were taken to create a professional civil service system. Indeed, a unified China requires an ideology that endorses the existence of a large bureaucracy. Only a complex governmental organization could hold the country together, given its diverse local traditions and cultures; the lack, until recently, of modern communications and transportation system; the segmented rather than nationally integrated economic system; and the huge population. Not surprisingly, the Western ideology which emerged dominant out of the chaotic warlord period in China was Leninism—essentially an ideology of organization.

Also not surprisingly, under Communist rule the bureaucratic ethic has been elaborated and supported primarily by bureaucrats, particularly those responsible for running the Chinese Communist party apparatus. Foremost among these was Liu Shao-ch'i, once designated Mao's successor but purged during the Cultural Revolution. [See articles on the Cultural Revolution in Section II, below.—Ed.] Essentially, one of the "crimes" for which Mao condemned Liu was his taking power away from Mao and lodging it in the party organization—that is, of ruling through institutions rather than men. Liu supposedly also championed other bureaucratic interests: hierarchy, discipline, career, recruitment based on merit. Although Liu has departed from the scene, a central concern of China's rulers . . . remained the problem to which Liu had devoted his life: how to build an effective party organization.

Totalitarian Beliefs

Yet one other belief system demands attention—totalitarianism. This creed deals with the ideal relationship between state and society. It advocates a total penetration of society by the government, with no areas of autonomy and freedom remaining. A willful dictator makes use of all the control levers at his disposal—political parties, the propaganda apparatus, the police and army, the educational network, commercial enterprises—to remake the society in his image. The whole nation comes to reflect its ruler: his fears, his hopes, abilities and emotions. "Politics takes command" is how [former Defense Minister] Lin [Piao] approvingly describes this situation.

Advocates of the totalitarian state have two basic aims. They desire to pulverize their society, isolating each individual so he becomes vulnerable to political control. This is achieved by creating an atmosphere of uncertainty, fear or terror, thereby making people feel helpless against the state. Second, they desire to build a strong state, particularly an omnipotent executive. These two aims focus upon power; indeed, the essence of the totalitarian mentality is its unquenchable thirst for power. Lin reflected this mentality in a remarkably candid speech:

> Never forget political power—always have it in mind. Once you forget political power, you forget politics and the fundamental views of Marxism. Consequently you swerve toward economism [the technological ethic in our terms], anarchism [the revolutionary ethic in our terms], and daydreaming. . . .
> What is political power? Sun Yat-sen believed it to be the management of the affairs of the masses. But he did not understand that political power is an instrument by which one class oppresses another. . . . I would put it as: political power is the power to suppress.

Three types of people appear to support a totalitarian state in China:

1. Those who believe such a political system is the best way to transform the society rapidly. The speeches of Lin suggest he may be, in part, an adherent of this view. Such people derive their inspiration not only from the forced industrialization of the Russian people under Stalin, but also draw upon indigenous doctrines and historical examples of how state power arises and should be organized, particularly the legalist philosophy and the examples of China under strong, willful emperors.

2. The few bureaucrats whose power is directly enhanced under totalitarian rule tend to support its philosophy. Thus, it is not surprising that the repudiated head of the secret police apparatus, K'ang Sheng, and the head of the public security apparatus, Hsieh Fu-chih, emerged as pivotal supporters of Mao during the Cultural Revolution.

3. The "inner court"—the people closest to the national leader who do not have a power base of their own but who share in his power and glory—has a vested interest in constantly expanding the prerogatives of the chief executive. Perhaps this helps to explain why Mao's wife Chiang Ch'ing, his apparent chief aide, Ch'en Po-ta and ideologues, such as Yao Wen-yüan, who had no independent, high bureaucratic position, have been the most enthusiastic advocates of the adulation of Chairman Mao: changing the party constitution to focus upon Mao; distributing a copy of Mao's sayings to every Chinese citizen; revising the performing arts in China so all plots pay homage to Mao's thought; and so on. By making Mao a demigod, those who are closest to him increase their own power vis-à-vis the bureaucracy, and they may be able to trade upon their proximity to Mao to retain influence after his death.

The Distinctiveness of China

These five belief systems come in conflict on some matters, but reinforce each other on others. For example, the tradi-

tional and revolutionary systems embody radically different
visions of the ideal society, but they both stress that man is
a social being, advocate the cultivation of a total man and
envision man in nature, not over it. The traditional and technological beliefs envision different ideal relationships between man and nature, but both place a premium on education. The totalitarian and bureaucratic beliefs stress the role
of the state in ordering society, but the totalitarian desire for
unchecked state power contrasts with the bureaucratic desire
for the rule of law.

Note some other ways in which aspects of these sets of
values overlap. Both the traditional and bureaucratic beliefs
esteem authority, hierarchy and discipline. Both the bureaucratic and technological ethics value specialization, competence and regularity. The traditional, revolutionary and
bureaucratic beliefs prize man's capacity to order society
through his innate talents. The revolutionary and totalitarian doctrines aim at a radical transformation of society.
It is precisely because of the overlap between these beliefs
that the adherents of each are able to form coalitions.

So, China contains a mix of these five sets of beliefs. But
how does this distinguish China from other countries? First,
two belief systems that are strong in the West and in former
Western colonies are almost absent in China: (1) theocratic
beliefs (except Chinese Buddhism) which stress the importance of the relationship between man and a supernatural
being; (2) liberal democratic beliefs which place a premium
upon individual procedural liberties and which value a diverse, pluralistic society. Neither strand of thought flourished
in China before the Western impact, and the thin reeds that
sprouted from Western seeds were cut by the Communists.

The second distinctively Chinese aspect of these values
are the historical memories associated with each. The traditional system is clearly identified with the moments of national greatness and therefore not easily rejected; the technological ethic is identified with the West and therefore only
reluctantly accepted—indeed, most easily accepted when

shown to be Chinese. Proponents of the revolutionary ideology identify the modern bureaucratic ethic with the conduct of the old Chinese Mandarinate (in fact, they differ), and therefore are deeply suspicious of it. The revolutionary ethic has special appeal to Chinese youth, for it is associated with some of the heroic movements of youth in modern China—the May Fourth movement or the resistance to Japan, for example—and with many of the legendary, romantic heroes of ancient Chinese history. Finally, it is possible that the weakness of the liberal democratic tradition and the lack of familiarity with Hitler's and Stalin's barbarism made totalitarianism somewhat less of a specter to the Chinese—initially, at least, before they personally experienced the harshness of Mao's dictatorship.

This leads to the final distinctive aspect of the five belief systems in China. The "mix" is different. The revolutionary belief system currently enjoys a strength unmatched elsewhere in the world, except perhaps in Algeria and Cuba, where it also receives official support. The continued albeit diminished vitality of the traditional system, although different from the traditional values of other countries, makes China somewhat comparable to other nations embarking upon industrialization. The totalitarian impulse, wedded to the revolutionary ethic, enjoys influence where it counts in the short run: at the top. The bureaucratic ethic was a specific object of attack during the height of the Cultural Revolution in 1966-67, but by 1970, it appeared that the attack upon it had met with failure. And, as for the past hundred years, the world continues to expect the imminent assertion of the technological ethic in China, confident that the signs point to its emergence as a dominant force after the current transition.

What is distinctive about China, then, is that *these* are the major belief systems at present and, more important, that none is dominant. When we ask about China's future, what we really are asking is: What will be the value-mix in the years ahead? Will any belief system emerge dominant?

Or will China remain in convulsion, without consensus, plagued by deep cleavages over basic values?

WHAT IT MEANS TO BE CHINESE [2]

I began to become aware of being Chinese at the age of three when my mother told me stories or sang folk songs about great emperors and ancient heroes and famous men of letters—about China's superior culture. I had no knowledge of foreigners, but I grew up believing that foreigners were barbarians.

I was growing up in Shanghai when I got my first look at a real foreigner. At that time, the city had special areas marked off as "foreign concessions," patrolled by helmeted and (to me) fierce-looking foreign soldiers. I also noticed many lovely parks and buildings. Some of them had signs announcing: "Dogs and Chinese not allowed."

Perhaps no voices are more foreign to an American than those of the Chinese. The two peoples are poles apart—separated by such a vast cultural, historic and psychological chasm that it is hardly surprising that Americans have so much trouble grasping that elusive sense of "Chinese-ness." Where a Westerner thinks in terms of *I*, a Chinese is apt to think of *we*. Where Western logic tends toward the absolutes of either/or, Chinese reasoning is based on the more harmonious blend of both/and. And if a primary gauge of Western civilization lies in its level of technical achievements and material affluence, the measure of Chinese society as Chinese see it lies in collective ethics and social organization.

China and the United States, in short, are separated by much more than geography—with the result that, more often than not, they have regarded each other with misunderstanding, distrust and hostility. But now, after a prolonged and bitter era in the relations between these two nations, a President of the United States . . . [has embarked] on a precedent-shattering journey to Peking. And thus an effort toward bridging the gap of mutual misunderstanding between 200 million Americans and 800 million Chinese has suddenly become more essential than ever before.

[2] From article in *Newsweek*. 79:36-9. F. 21, '72. Copyright Newsweek, Inc. 1972, reprinted by permission.

For foreigners, a persistent stumbling block to understanding the Chinese is the sheer magnitude of the subject. In all, the Chinese form the largest tribe on the face of the earth, a single massive and, in some ways, an astonishingly cohesive grouping that constitutes nearly a quarter of all mankind. Their rich traditions span virtually the whole of man's recorded history—and reach even beyond that to the misty realm of legend and myth. Through more than three millennia, records of China's existence unroll like an endless scroll through twenty-four dynastic cycles. Little wonder that one American missionary was moved to complain: "The trouble with Chinese history is that there is altogether too much of it."

I was taught that it was virtuous to be useful to society, to curb one's individual desires, to get along well with others. To be selfish was considered bad; to be disloyal was considered bad; to be unkind was considered very bad.

To ignore the impact of China's complex and frequently glorious history would be to miss a theme that is central to the Chinese makeup. For it is from history that each Chinese derives his strongest sense of identity. And while a deep attachment to cultural roots can hardly be said to be a uniquely Chinese characteristic, certainly no other people has expressed a devotion to its peculiar traditions for so long or on such a pervasive scale. Whatever their individual qualities or quirks, their circumstances or political allegiance, whether they live in China itself or are scattered to distant lands, pride in the Chinese cultural heritage links all Chinese. As Li Cho-ming, vice chancellor of the Chinese University of Hong Kong, explains it: "I look back on Chinese history, and I think there really has never been anything like China. . . . Basically, ours is a history of continuous civilized life that has gone on longer than any others. And this is something every Chinese realizes and is proud of."

In fact, for all the bewildering variations within Chinese society, China long ago achieved a startling degree of cultural homogeneity. A system of philosophical values and social

attitudes became so thoroughly entrenched as to be the un-
questioned norms. And despite the numerous inequities of
the old system, the essence of traditional China's philosophical outlook remained pragmatic and humanistic. The doctrine that "people come first before all else" is not a concept
one would necessarily expect to be cherished in a society that
traditionally has had a superabundance of people. Yet, as
Professor Ping-ti Ho of the University of Chicago points out:
"No other major culture in the world so consistently relied
on man rather than God . . . a reliance on the human spirit
and will, faith in his ability to solve his own difficulties—that
is the Chinese attitude toward mankind."

I was a good son and never dared to do or say anything to
provoke my father's wrath. Once, after I got a zero on a math exam,
he bent me over a chair and spanked me with a hand of iron. I
felt greatly disgraced and concentrated on redeeming the blight I
felt I had brought on my family's name.

As with other countries, China's social organization reflected its particular environment. As Harvard Sinologist
John K. Fairbank wrote: "Chinese man has been so crowded
upon the soil among his fellows that he is also a most socially
minded human being, ever conscious of the interplay of per-
sonalities and social conventions around him. . . . He is seldom in all his life beyond earshot of other people." Quite
understandably then, the Confucian ethic that dominated
and shaped Chinese society for some two thousand years was
preoccupied with human relationships, defining the rank,
title, role and duties of each member within the social structure in precise detail.

At the core of Chinese social thinking was the family
structure, which in China meant the extended family or clan.
The huge family with multiple generations living together
in a single compound was something to which all Chinese
aspired. In reality, however, relatively few families possessed
the wealth to support such a large, expensive establishment.
Still, it was achieved often enough to remain the ideal, and
many Chinese today still remember it well. "Our entire six-

hundred-member clan, like many others in China at that time, formed a distinct social unit," recalls *Newsweek*'s Hong Kong correspondent, Sydney Liu.

We had some 1,200 acres of farm land altogether, which constituted the resources for a mutual-welfare fund. A portion of the income from these lands was used for the repair and upkeep of three family temples and numerous tombs, for the care of sick and poor within the clan or to subsidize the education of young clan members. A committee of elders elected by the entire clan ran the fund—and their decisions were indisputably final.

In such a system, the highest virtues were ancestral veneration, respect for elders and duty to the group. "We were taught as children that filial piety was the most important virtue," remembers P. C. Woo, a Hong Kong lawyer in his mid-fifties.

This was followed by instruction that we should never do anything that would bring dishonor to the family name. That would include acting dishonestly, behaving rudely in public, drinking too much and smoking opium (a lot of people smoked opium when I was a young boy). The family ties were very strong but my family would not have expected a member to behave in a dishonest way in order to look after a kinsman—like offering a bribe to get one of them out of trouble. We were taught to be honest first—and discreet.

The subordination of the individual to the welfare of the family, however, did not mean that an individual counted for nothing in old China. Rather, the Chinese tended to regard each person as a valuable element of the group and judged individual conduct and achievement as they reflected on the group as a whole. Nor was the status of women, though it was bleak enough in traditional Chinese society, wholly without redeeming features. For while the eldest male in the family was absolute boss, the ranking female usually had plenty to say about what went on within her household. Women of lesser status in the family were expected to wait on *fu-ren* (the mistress) hand and foot, and for them the only real hope was to bear sons and survive long enough so that they, too, would become that most powerful of female figures—the mother-in-law. . . .

Like a mirror of the family, the Chinese political structure has always been basically authoritarian. But it was not necessarily a system of blind obedience or passive acceptance. For Chinese tradition also sanctioned the right to rebel against unjust authority and, indeed, some scholars have sought to view Chinese history as a long series of peasant revolts. But if rulers were toppled for failure to measure up to accepted standards of virtuous conduct, the Confucian system itself went unchallenged. Conserved by a ruling class of scholar-officials steeped in the classics, sustained by collective pressures toward social conformity, the old system endured until the modern era.

Before the nineteenth century, in fact, there was nothing in their racial experience that might have jogged Chinese into considering an alternative to Confucianism. They were all but totally isolated from the civilization of the West. And in their neighbors around the periphery of the Chinese Empire, they perceived only lesser cultures that were no match for the richness of China's own philosophic, literary and artistic patterns. Over time, the notions that China was the Middle Kingdom, the center of the world, "all under heaven" (or, at least, all that a civilized Chinese need concern himself with) took firm hold. The Middle Kingdom was not a nation-state in the modern sense since, at that time, the Chinese could hardly conceive of their land as just another country among many. As British journalist and author Dennis Bloodworth has observed: "The Chinese . . . did not think of China as the British thought of Britain, but as Christians thought of Christendom." With their sense of moral and cultural superiority, it was self-evident to the Chinese that those who embraced China's culture were the enlightened, those who did not were barbarians.

As a result, the Chinese were totally unprepared for the Western onslaught in the nineteenth century. Just as the West came to China ignorant of the great civilization it was plundering, the Chinese failed to perceive the challenge posed by these "barbarians." China's emperors had seen

European visitors not as ambassadors from equal nations but simply as new envoys in a long procession of vassals bearing tribute. What the Chinese could not comprehend was that the intruding Western civilization might rival and in some ways—particularly in weaponry and technology—surpass their own. Thus, when the Europeans—and the Japanese—began to successfully carve up the mainland, the comfortable illusions of superiority that had reassured the Chinese throughout their history were shattered.

When I was a schoolboy in China I was oh so proud of my cultural heritage. Yet I was also sad. For even then, I had this great sadness because modern China was so weak.

Disbelief gave way to bewilderment, then bitter shame. Often, the Chinese responded to the new Western presence with a characteristic ambivalence.

Western material civilization was held in awe by almost all Chinese [Sydney Liu recalls]. Anything foreign-made had to be good. The goal of almost every Chinese student was to go abroad to learn how to build factories, to make weapons and communications systems to enable China once again to become a power in the world. Yet a Chinese was not to trust any foreigners. The idea was to use foreign techniques, but to retain the traditional Chinese ideals.

Underscoring this effort was a sense of suppressed anger, the visceral rage of the proud who had been humbled. Xenophobia flourished. To the Chinese, it seemed as if outsiders used the very term *Chinese* to imply "backwardness" and "inferiority." The goal of rebuilding and unifying China became the common aim of every Chinese political movement, though there was great dispute over who was going to lead the nation to salvation. Still, in the autumn of 1949, when a triumphant Mao Tse-tung proclaimed that "the Chinese people have stood up," the message was instantly grasped by every Chinese. And of late, the emergence of China on the international diplomatic scene has been cheered by most Chinese as proof of their nation's restored pride.

In the final analysis, the feeling of Chinese-ness clearly transcends nationalism and politics. There are, for example, some nineteen million Chinese outside China's territories, living in nearly half the world's nations. Some may be descendants of families who have been abroad for generations and whose direct ties to China may be tenuous at best. Some may now give their primary allegiance to their adopted land and would not consider a return to China for anything longer than a brief visit. Some may find the ideology of the regime, or the regimentation of the society, uncongenial to their own values and tastes. Some may be appalled by the periodic turmoil that has buffeted Maoist China—particularly the assault on historic treasures during the Cultural Revolution. But they retain the hope for a unified, strong China as a symbol of their own heritage and pride. "Now China has pride," said Professor Ping-ti Ho as he thought back on his youth, when the calendar was pocked by official "days of humiliation" to mark yet another national catastrophe. "At least now—today—no Chinese need observe a day of national humiliation."

COMING OF AGE IN COMMUNIST CHINA [3]

From time immemorial, the family has come first in China. It was Confucius who taught that every Chinese owed his primary loyalty to kith and kin. And Mencius, the fourth century B.C. sage, wrote: "The substance of humanity is to serve one's parents." In the space of two short decades, however, Mao Tse-tung has sought to change all that. As part of his vast experiment in remolding the Chinese masses in his revolutionary image, he has initiated a whole new approach to child rearing, education, and relations between the sexes— all with the goal of making the family serve the state. . . .

Like the Puritan youngsters in Colonial America, the eighteen million children born each year in China are virtually weaned on the state's all-pervasive religion. Even though a

[3] From article in *Newsweek*. 79:44-7. F. 21, '72. Copyright Newsweek, Inc. 1972, reprinted by permission.

shortage of jobs keeps many women from working, millions of Chinese mothers do labor in factories or businesses and till the soil alongside their husbands. As a result, their children's early years are for the most part spent in day-care centers, or, on the communes, under the traditional tutelage of grandmothers. [See the next selection, "How the Oldest Civilization in the World Brings Up Its Youngest Members," for an eyewitness report on child rearing in China.—Ed.]

For the children in a city day-care center, it is not entirely a life without mother. Even though the babies are toilet-trained, bathed and taught to make their beds by the day-care staff, the mothers are allowed time off from work to nurse their children. Moreover, the youngsters spend evenings and weekends in the warm embrace of their families. Nonetheless, their early group experience conditions Chinese children to seek the approval of their peers—a prerequisite for successful existence in the Maoist state. And political indoctrination begins in earnest in nursery school, where such plays as "The Little Truck Driver Goes to Peking to See Chairman Mao" and songs such as "Happy Tidings of Victory from Indochina" are a staple of a child's daily diet.

Once it has begun, such indoctrination never stops. "In kindergarten," says Ruth Sidel, a New York psychiatric social worker who visited China last year, "children are taught to be the 'inheritors of the Socialist cause.' " Their games are couched in political terms: as they climb over chairs, crawl through hoops and cross a play bridge, they are told this represents the hardships of Mao's Long March. "In a tug of war that I saw in a Canton kindergarten," recalls civil rights leader Hosea Williams, "the teacher chided the losing team, 'You're going to be the imperialists.' " By the time a child is in elementary school, he has become "a Little Red Soldier" —the still-functioning younger version of the Red Guards— and spends part of his day in the schoolyard pretending to shoot at cutouts of Uncle Sam. Even the academic curriculum is politically tinted. A typical elementary school math problem runs: "473 students out of 500 volunteered to go to the countryside and do productive labor. What percentage volunteered to do so?"

But while the basic Chinese curriculum includes a hefty chunk of Chairman Mao's thoughts, a number of US educators who have recently traveled to the mainland point out that it also encompasses mathematics, geography, art and literature, politics, the Chinese language and even foreign languages—with English the most prevalent. . . . Even here, however, Chinese teachers find ways to inject politics into the curriculum. A recent visitor recalls watching ten-year-olds learning two English sentences: "We have boundless love of Chairman Mao" and "My brother is in the People's Liberation Army." Aside from the emphasis on propaganda, however, teaching methods are still old-fashioned. "Despite talk about teaching reforms," says Massachusetts Institute of Technology political scientist Susan Shirk, "it will be some time before rote learning and reciting are replaced by the informal give-and-take the leadership wants."

Still, the Chinese have instituted some revolutionary changes in education. "They are trying to eliminate grades and competition," notes Yale Professor Arthur Galston. "Exams are used to let the student know what he doesn't know and tell the professor where he failed as a teacher." Moreover, the schools apply the group-critique method that is so much a part of all Chinese Communist life. It is accepted practice for students to break down into groups at the end of the term and review everything—teachers, curriculum, fellow students; they debate what was right and wrong, and try to correct problems before starting a new year.

As might be expected, the goal of education in an underdeveloped country like China is primarily practical, and all students are made to feel like apprentices. "In a kindergarten I visited," recalled Helen Rosen, a New York audiologist, "children made cardboard boxes which were sent to a factory, filled with crayons and then sent back to the school." And University of Wisconsin graduate student Ken Levin added, "In one primary school in Nanking, the kids were building air filters for trucks, and in some rural areas the students are constructing the school buildings themselves." Every high school graduate must put in a stretch of "serving the people" —by working in a factory or a commune or by joining the army for as much as three years. Even then, his peers must approve his performance and recommend him for further schooling before university gates will open. "If you want to go to college," says Rhoads Murphey, director of the University of Michigan's Center for Chinese Studies, "the best thing to say is, 'I want to be the best peasant, work hardest and learn from the other peasants.' And then you must do just that. The person who succeeds is the one who volunteers first for the most barren and difficult place."

Despite all this, the life of youth in "New China" has not changed in at least one important way—most boys and girls in their early twenties are still virgins. Chinese sexual mores have always been fiercely conservative, but even so, modern Chinese seem more sorely inhibited than their parents were. While couples may stroll hand in hand or seek the rare privacy of a park bench, that is as far as they go until marriage. Any would-be Lothario who tried to play the field would be mercilessly scorned by his fellows. "If you play around with girls, nobody will trust you," says one recent refugee from the mainland.

Since few Chinese dare risk public disapproval by marrying before the officially approved ages of twenty-five for women and . . . [twenty-eight to thirty] for men, they must endure years of sexual privation. "When you ask Chinese adolescents about their love life," says Jean Leclerc du Sablon, the Agence France Presse correspondent in Peking, "they blush and stammer: 'We play a lot of sports and work hard to build the country.' " Some visitors are not totally convinced by all this and suspect with Michigan's Professor Murphey that "there is a good deal of funny business going on behind the haymow." Perhaps. But the fact is that the Chinese go to great lengths to avoid any public sexual provocation. Young women wear baggy trousers, hide their brightly col-

ored blouses beneath drab "unisex" jackets and do not use
makeup. . . .

The social taboos on romantic involvement lend some
credibility to the official version of how boy meets girl—on
the job. "Like marries like," says French journalist François
Debré. "An interpreter will very likely have an interpreter
wife, and a doctor will have a doctor husband."

Even after marriage, moreover, a Chinese couple finds
that the government and party are actively involved in their
life. Acutely aware of its population problem, China encourages parents to have only two children—a policy it pro-
motes mainly by indirect means. To begin with, since the
average Chinese family is usually limited to a two-room
apartment (and must often share kitchen and bath facilities
with other families), more children mean less space. As a
further incentive to parents to restrict their families, the
government sanctions abortions and sells condoms throughout the country (as cheaply as two for a penny). And even
though the most commonly used female contraceptives are
the standard Western birth-control pill and intrauterine devices, the Chinese have a special version of the pill—a sheet
of saturated rice paper that is eaten in stamp-size bites.

Like the government, the neighbors are authorized in-
truders in China. "Street and Lane Committees" in the cities
and "Team Authorities" in the communes hold regular
meetings to examine not only political attitudes but intimate
marriage details as well. "They may begin by asking details
about your earnings and your possessions," recalls a refugee
now living in Hong Kong, "and end by asking about your
attitude toward your wife." (If a couple wants to get di-
vorced, they must first discuss their difficulties with the neigh-
borhood committee and get its approval.) Yet the Chinese
seem to accept such inquisitions as a normal part of life. And
judging by reports from recent visitors, they maintain a
tightly knit and peaceful family life. "There is no generation
gap," notes Keiko Saino, a Japanese woman who recently

visited China. "One of their values is the 'combination of three'—the aged, the young and those in the middle."

There is, as well, a noticeable new harmony between men and women, who have developed a relationship that Western advocates of women's liberation could well envy. Casting aside chauvinist terms, married couples refer to each other as *ai-ren,* a word meaning "sweetheart" or "lover," rather than as husband or wife. Chinese men and women share some household chores, the shopping, the budgeting. And the autocratic husband seems to be a thing of the past. Yet, the Chinese have clearly not obliterated all sexual roles. Says Nobel prize-winning physicist Chen Ning Yang: "Roles are still differentiated." And Harvard graduate student Kay Johnson adds: "There are discrepancies in jobs—engineering is considered a man's job, for example, while women staff day-care centers and teach elementary school."

However much China may have closed the traditional gap between the sexes and improved the lot of its people, many aspects of life in Mao's China are patently abhorrent to Americans. Some, like Hosea Williams, are appalled by all the ideological saturation. "It's the children growing up who worry me," he says. "Nobody can be taught to hate like that and not be affected." Yet many American educators have noted that Chinese children seem to have few neurotic hang-ups—and they attribute this mental health to the sense of acceptance the children derived from belonging to the group. Other visitors have been disturbed by the blatant snooping of the street committees into private lives. But unlike Americans, the Chinese have never made a sharp distinction between *private* and *public.* "The thing for Westerners to remember," says a China expert, "is that although Mao has wrought many drastic changes in the Chinese way of life, he has not tampered with the Chinese sense of groupness. The Chinese have always felt part of something larger than themselves, and today that something is the state."

HOW THE OLDEST CIVILIZATION IN THE WORLD BRINGS UP ITS YOUNGEST MEMBERS [4]

"My baby is as happy and as plump as a sparrow. I pick him up at the nursery on Saturday afternoon and return him on Monday morning. If I am away working, he simply stays at the nursery."

Li Huh, an interpreter with Luxingshe, the state travel agency that arranges all tours for "foreign guests" (tourists inside mainland China), gave a radiant smile.

"My son is beautifully cared for and loved. I speak two foreign languages and my country needs my services. It would be crazy for me to sit at home for ten years looking after one baby!"

Huh—which means joy or festivity—was thirty-two years old, a tall woman with a mischievous grin. With her shoulder-length braids held in rubber bands and her well-scrubbed face minus any makeup, she looked at least ten years younger.

It was late in the summer of 1971 and we were sitting in a train going from Peking to Shia Chia Ch'uan, the capital of Hopei province. This was my second visit to the People's Republic of China. In 1965 I had managed to join a tourist group going there, by giving my occupation as housewife and an address in my native Australia. Actually, at the time, I was living in the United States with my American husband and working for the San Francisco *Examiner*. Thus, I became the first American newspaperwoman to get into mainland China.

Now I was there again, this time with a Canadian tour organized by the University of British Columbia. Huh and I sat in our upholstered private compartment, drinking tea at a small table by an open window, shouting a little over the wind and noise.

Huh, dressed in the garb of the modern Chinese city woman—a plain white cotton blouse and loose gray slacks—

[4] From article by Lisa Hobbs, journalist. *Parents Magazine & Better Family Living.* 47:52-3+. Ap. '72. Reprinted by permission.

continued our discussion of child care and family life in the new China.

"Very often grandparents take care of their grandchildren. As you know, everyone in our society works; everyone contributes something. If my mother were alive she would take care of my son. As for my mother-in-law, she does not live in Peking. Sometimes an elderly neighbor, a sort of substitute grandmother, will care for a child. But if no one in the family is available, we have plenty of nurseries."

I asked Huh if she ever worried about the dangers of "institutionalizing" her child. Her frank and pretty face looked puzzled. What did I mean, dangers? I explained that often in institutions there was insufficient staff to give children the attention they needed at the time they needed it. As a result, such children could experience confusion about their own identity and feel deprived.

Huh burst into laughter—not out of scorn, but sheer amusement.

"You have seen our children," she said good-humoredly. "Would you say they seem deprived?"

I readily admitted that, of all the youngsters I had observed in various parts of the world, Chinese children certainly appeared to be among the best nourished, loved, and cared for.

After a number of visits to crèches (state-run, day-care nurseries), primary schools, hospitals, and public places during a month-long tour which took me to eight major Chinese cities and many towns and villages, I had formed the clear impression that the people of China truly regard their babies as their country's most precious product. And this love of children is not in conflict with the pressure for population control—a major government concern for more than a decade.

The annual population growth in China today is estimated at about eighteen million, and government policy has set two children as the ideal family. I was told that although it was surely understandable if a peasant family had four children (sons and daughters provide welcome hands in farming), for a college-trained, urban citizen to have more than two children would reflect a reprehensible lack of sensitivity toward the country's problem of overpopulation.

One tall, bespectacled man of about thirty put it this way: "The love of children is in the bones of our people." He went on to explain, however, that couples would not well express that love in the interest of the country by having large families. "Besides," he added, "it is bad for the mother's health and the country's educational system to have a lot of children." His reference to education reflects the facts that China suffers from a chronic shortage of both teachers and classrooms.

The great care and energy devoted to the raising of children is one of the most striking features of life in China today. Prenatal clinics are widespread. I was told that they offered classes in painless labor and delivery, although I saw no evidence of this myself. Postnatal clinics offer examinations at six weeks, six months, and a year. Employed women—and all women do some sort of work—are given two months maternity leave with full pay. When the mother returns to work, the child is usually taken to the crèche provided by the factory or office. Breast feeding is the norm, and nursing breaks, as required, are given throughout the day.

"It has worked very well for me," said Lo Yien-feng, a member of the administrative committee of the ten-acre People's Cultural Park in downtown Canton. Yien-feng, a tiny figure in loose navy denim slacks and pale blue shirt, lived four miles from work and there was no crèche within the park. But there was one nearby. She nursed the child there just before starting work, again during her hour lunch time, then after work.

I asked, as a former nursing mother myself, if this were not a tiring schedule, and Yien-feng readily admitted she was finding it so. Still, she intended to make the routine succeed because she took great pleasure in nursing her little girl, though she planned to do it only for five or six months instead of the usual year.

In the rural areas, the crèche or nursery is often located near the "Homes of Respect for the Aged," so that during the day children are cared for by real or substitute grandparents.

There appeared to be no typical dinner arrangements. Some husbands and wives work together in the same factories. The bigger plants always have cafeterias, in which case a couple might eat supper there together before picking up their child and returning home. Couples who live in one of the new housing developments are likely to eat in the communal dining room, or cook in their own kitchen, shared usually by three other families.

Often, the evening meal for a younger working couple is prepared by a retired woman who lives in the same apartment block. For, even after retirement, the elderly are expected to perform simple daily tasks which give them a strong sense of still being useful, of being contributing members of the community.

At the age of two the child goes into a nursery; later, a kindergarten. All, of course, are state run. There is no such thing as private property or private enterprise. Nowhere, in either city or country, did I see any evidence of deprivation, such as many in the West expected.

I found several reasons that might explain the high standards of child welfare in China despite the changes in traditional family life.

One is that, while the legal age for marriage is 18 for women and 20 for men, the "advised" age is 25 for women and . . . [28 to 30] for men. Encouraging late marriages is not so difficult as it might first seem to Westerners, since there are no social pressures pushing young people into marriage. There is no sexy advertising, no competitiveness in clothes or personal beauty. In these later marriages, couples regard their responsibilities very seriously. For the first time in China's history, young people are allowed to choose their own husbands and wives rather than accept a spouse selected by their parents.

Once a couple has reached the legal or "advised" age and decides to marry, the two notify their work units, receive approval in most cases, and then apply for housing. To marry, they simply go to the local police station and register as a married couple.

The newly registered husband and wife usually invite friends in for tea and sweets and make a public declaration, the wording of which they choose themselves. They might vow, for example, "to practice self-criticism within marriage to become better builders of the new society."

The serious attitude toward marriage is reinforced by the fact that divorce is discouraged and, if children are involved, difficult to obtain. All couples seeking divorce must first go through a reconciliation court.

"It is usual for a couple to have a baby within a year or so of marriage," said Huh. "After all, we sometimes wait a long while to marry and so want to start our families right away." The majority of babies, therefore, are planned for and wanted.

In China, all work related to child care has a high social and economic status. Women involved in it feel deeply that they are caring for the builders of the new China, and seem imbued with a sense of vocation and dedication. They are warm, firm, serene yet outspoken. In both the crèches and nursery schools there appears to be one nurse or teacher for every six children and, at kindergarten level, one for every eight youngsters.

That much-discussed aspect of child care in our society—toilet-training—has little meaning in China. There is no emphasis or concern about it at all, an attitude that appears to have remarkably efficient results. Babies wear diapers until they can toddle about, after which they merely imitate their older playmates. This is possible because the overalls that the young children wear are very baggy, the bagginess hiding the fact that the pants are not closed at the back between waist and crotch. With no buttons to be undone, or straps to be lowered, little people can look after themselves merely by squatting. In nursery play yards, even along the main boulevards of the cities, there are many old-fashioned chamber pots and the children use them freely and without self-consciousness.

There are other factors that contribute to the atmosphere of serenity in which children are raised. Not only is the working mother often free of the normal cooking chores that await the working mother in North America at the end of a day in the office or factory, but it is also the norm for all working women to send out the laundry. Laundry services, particularly in the vast new housing complexes, are exceedingly cheap. Furthermore, the children's nurseries and kindergartens provide any change of clothing that might be required during the day.

As for household work, there is little indeed to be done—for housing is extremely confining and humble by Western standards. Most Chinese cities are centuries old, labyrinths of winding alleys and stone walls with one-room dwellings opening directly onto the streets. The new apartments are simply single rooms, twelve by sixteen feet, not much larger and sometimes smaller than the older dwellings. But they are bright, clean, dry, have steam heat and are eagerly sought after. Time and again I was shown one of these apartments with great pride. The nearby kitchen, with a concrete floor and three butane gas ranges, is shared by four families. There is cold running water into twin concrete sinks but no hot water.

The Chinese are scrupulously clean, despite the fact that if one does not care to go to the communal shower and bathrooms, one must wash from a bowl within one's own room.

(This single room appeared to be the standard for housing in the overcrowded cities. In rural villages, however, where there are often four or five children to a family, many houses are consequently more spacious; a large kitchen-family room in the center may be adjoined by bedrooms and storage rooms.)

As the working mother in the city has no cooking or housework to do, parents are free to spend their evening hours enjoying the company of their children. Pleasures in China are very simple; Western social life, with its round of visits and dinner parties, is unknown. Without television or automobiles, parents seem to derive the utmost pleasure from a simple night stroll, playing ball in the park, or going to an occasional movie, always accompanied by their children.

This relaxed attitude undergoes a marked change as the child progresses through kindergarten to primary school. Because the aim of education in China is to produce "a skilled worker with a Socialist conscience," there is no learning for its own sake. Nor is education seen as a way to better oneself or increase income and social prestige.

The rulers of China believe they can consolidate their system only if manual work is invested with value and dignity. This precept, which is held through the university level, is put into practice in kindergarten. And it was at this early stage of schooling that I noted two substantial differences in the education process between the time of my first visit in 1965 and the present. The first difference is that in 1965 there was no emphasis on physical labor or community involvement until at least middle, or late, primary school. The second—particularly interesting to us in the West—is that although the political indoctrination of children is as intense today as then, its tone and targets have changed greatly.

During my 1965 visit there was not a performance given by kindergartners that I saw which was not directed at so-called American imperialism. Today, the "wickedness" of the West is far less emphasized; now the stress is definitely inward, on urging the young people to solve their country's problems, particularly their economic ones, internally.

But the process of educating children mainly to be good citizens of the state has not been a simple task. "Many teachers cling to the notion that education is a means of developing the intellect rather than a means of developing a Socialist worker," said Madame Niu, principal of the Nanking Chenhsien primary school.

Are children encouraged to criticize their teachers? Absolutely, Madame beamed, so much so that many teachers complained that being a teacher these days in China is "unlucky." The basis of the problem was simple. Many teachers come from intellectual backgrounds, and yet they are trying to educate the children of workers, peasants, and soldiers. How could people from such a middle-class, bourgeois background really understand the lives of these children?

The problem Madame Niu posed sounded reminiscent of the communication gap in the United States between ghetto children and middle-class teachers. The solution to this problem in China is to have all teachers leave the classroom and live for a year or so in rural areas, working the land and living with the poorest of the peasants in an effort to gain insights into the daily realities of their lives.

Such a system sounds harsh indeed to a Westerner. Yet physical labor is not regarded as a punishment but as a means of reaching what's real, of ridding oneself of bureaucratic tendencies. It is not unlike the monastic idea of a retreat, a process of work, study, discussion, and purification.

By the time a Chinese youngster reaches high school, half of each day is devoted to classroom work, half to physical labor. Students weed the parks, sweep the streets, work in the marketplaces. At one school I visited the students made simple repairs of household goods. At another, they made door parts for the city bus system.

There are no examinations or graduation ceremonies on leaving high school. The relationship between student and teacher is so close that testing is felt to be neither necessary nor desirable. As one high school teacher said: "It is a simple fact that some children do not perform well in examinations but they are fine workers and good citizens. This is more important to us than theory on paper."

On leaving high school, all students become "workers." They must spend three to four years doing manual work before they can be considered for the university. Even then, they are chosen for further education only if they prove themselves to be politically active and have "a high level of political consciousness."

The lives of adolescents are, by American standards, extremely structured and restricted. Pleasures are simple: a picnic, perhaps, or a concert the students stage themselves. Three plain but nutritious meals are eaten daily. There are no snacks from slot machines, no jukeboxes, no automobiles or rock 'n' roll, no comics, no pornographic literature, no nude movies, no drinking, and no drugs.

Although contraceptives are available, the attitude towards sex among high school and university students is rigidly puritanical. One girl described premarital sex as "unthinkable." And a young man asked me if it were true that Western college girls were "morally loose." When I replied that a few were but most were not, he confided that even in China "in the rural areas where couples are used to marrying earlier, there is an occasional love child." But he said that in such a case, the couple would marry. I asked why, since abortions there are legal, and he replied that most Chinese did not care for abortions.

Life for a married couple is surely, by our standards, difficult in many ways. Work-enforced separations of husbands and wives—particularly those with highly specialized training—are not uncommon.

Should the state require a man's (or a woman's) services a thousand miles away from his partner's place of employment, that will be his legal domicile. One young woman I met, a physicist, has been married for three years and has a two-year-old son. The child lives with his grandmother while his mother works at a laboratory far from their home city. Separated couples like this one are given a month's vacation each year to spend together. But such unnatural separations exist for only two or three years. The state does not expect its young couples to be saints indefinitely, and if temptations to infidelity occur, the state will allow the couple to be reunited. Such a reunion, however, marks the fact that the couple is not of the steel that the state prizes most highly.

There are many elements in contemporary Chinese society that sound alien, even repugnant, to Westerners. But for the Chinese, it would seem that their leaders have effectively transferred the emotional investment people usually reserve for their own families to society as a whole.

While it is true that the sense of family appears to play a lesser role than formerly in the lives of young people, there is no visible evidence of loss or emotional deprivation among young or old. If a judgment were asked of me, I would have to say that, of the many countries I have visited, I have seen no other children who look forward to the future with a greater sense of purpose and confidence than these "young builders of the new society of China."

II. THE CULTURAL REVOLUTION

EDITOR'S INTRODUCTION

Of all the tumultuous events which have wracked China in the past two decades, perhaps none have appeared so startling, chaotic, and mystifying as the so-called Cultural Revolution. On the one hand, the Cultural Revolution appeared to be ideological fanaticism, an attack by Communist party zealots on what was known as the "four olds"—old ideas, old culture, old customs and old habits. The point presumably was to rid the society of "contaminated" bourgeois and Western influences which still remained among Chinese citizens. On the other hand, this national campaign, orchestrated and conducted by party chairman Mao Tse-tung, was a drive to purge the country of those who he felt opposed his ideas and vision for the future.

On another level, the Cultural Revolution was also a determined attempt by Mao to mold China and its people into the kind of Communist society he believed he was striving to achieve, a society in which—to put it most idealistically—all would work for the common good as visualized by the Communist party. In this sense it is important to regard Mao and his associates not only as political leaders but as the leading spirits in what has been called one of history's most ambitious attempts at social engineering.

So significant is the Cultural Revolution in terms of understanding contemporary China and Chinese communism that this compilation explores it in some depth. The first article, written while the Cultural Revolution was still sweeping China in 1967, describes what happened on a day-to-day basis. The second piece reprints a decree of the Central Committee of the Chinese Communist party concerning the Cultural Revolution. This document is interesting because it can be read as an instruction manual for the "Red Guards"—young Chinese who zealously and violently fought the "four olds" and who referred to Mao's now-famous little red book of political thoughts and aphorisms for inspiration and guidance.

The third article offers a nonpartisan retrospective survey of the Cultural Revolution so that the entire sweep of this social phenomenon can be seen. The fourth article, taken from *Problems of Communism* and written by the director of the East Asian Studies Center at Stanford University, presents a detailed analysis of the significance and meaning of the Cultural Revolution. The article notes that this upheaval was by no means an isolated occurrence and that from the very beginning of their regime the Communists had stressed the importance of changing the minds and perceptions of the people to fit the desired image—a herculean task but one which Mao believed had become an urgent need by the mid-1960s.

AS RED CHINA PLUNGES
DEEPER INTO CHAOS [1]
Reprinted from *U.S. News & World Report.*

Communist China, [in 1967] after months of internal upheaval, is fast approaching national disintegration. Complete chaos seems likely unless Mao Tse-tung calls a halt to his "revolution."

The purge and power struggle for leadership, which began in Peking over one year ago, have now enveloped almost the entire country. The political system no longer functions effectively. The machinery of government has broken down.

The only effective power base left is the army. So far, it has remained aloof from the strife, except to restore order in such cities as Canton and Wuhan when violence has become uncontrolled.

[1] From article in *U.S. News & World Report.* 63:36-8. O. 2, '67.

Most striking and evident is the effect on the economy. In China's richest agricultural provinces, peasants are neglecting their chores and ignoring orders. In key industrial cities, workers are abandoning their jobs and defying authorities.

Factories are closed, train schedules have been curtailed, ports are idled and harvests endangered—all as a result of Communist party leader Mao Tse-tung's call to China's people—780 million, by one recent estimate—to join a "Cultural Revolution." The outlook, according to diplomatic and intelligence sources in touch with Western officials, is for even worse conditions in the months ahead.

Trains That Don't Run

Hardest hit by the economic dislocation are communications and transport, services that were never too good. Strikes, sabotage of rolling stock and lack of proper maintenance have crippled the railroads which move most goods inside China.

Trains from Peking to Shanghai reportedly have been cut from two a day to four a week. The Shanghai-Canton run often takes 15 days instead of 2. On some days, in some areas, there is no train service at all. These suspensions and disruptions are pinching the flow of raw materials to factories and hampering delivery of finished goods.

One measure of the consequences: In August [1967], the volume of Chinese rail shipments to neighboring Hong Kong dropped nearly 80 percent.

Port operations have suffered, too. Turnaround time for ships in Shanghai harbor, normally 4 days, now is up to 12 days. Cargoes pile up on the docks.

Chinese exports and imports registered a slight decline in the first half of 1967, in contrast to steady increases in the past three years. The impact of the disorders is seen as likely to be cumulative, leading to a sharper drop in trade volume —and in foreign-exchange earnings.

Coal Output: Paralyzed

For months, countless strikes, walkouts and bloody clashes involving workers, juvenile Red Guards and troops have been upsetting industrial production.

Several blast furnaces reportedly have been destroyed at Anshan, source of half of the country's steel. Prolonged fighting has paralyzed Shansi's vital coal mines and has upset production in the largest petroleum fields in both the northwest and northeast.

Hundreds of workers have been killed or injured in the important textile mills of Szechwan. Output of machinery, equipment and vehicles has dropped off in such industrial centers as Shanghai, Wuhan and Mukden.

Few mines, factories or public utilities have been unaffected. Endless political demonstrations have lowered the productivity of workers. Young "revolutionary rebels" have assumed jobs they know nothing about. Industrial accidents have risen sharply.

Frightened managers' false reports on output probably have concealed the degree of industrial dislocation even from Chinese authorities, but it appears significant that Peking is making few production claims any more.

Slowdown—How Serious?

Some experts are convinced that the overall forward thrust of the economy has not yet been seriously slowed, arguing that removal of the dead hand of bureaucracy may have, in many cases, improved production. Others are less optimistic.

Conditions are equally confusing on the farms, where 80 percent of China's millions still make a precarious living with crude tools and primitive methods. From all accounts, the peasants are as dissatisfied with their lot as are industrial workers.

Peasants are accused of attacking collective storehouses, hiding grain and hoarding food, refusing to surrender rice levies to the state, skimping on field work and fleeing to the cities.

The weather has been reasonably good and this year's harvest may be at least average, but there is no certainty that granary areas will be willing—or able—to share with city residents and with provinces that normally fail to produce enough food for their own use.

Civil Disorder

Children let out of school a year ago to implement Mao Tse-tung's dream of a "pure" Communist society for China are refusing to return to their classrooms, and delinquency is rising. In some places, jails have been emptied and prisoners are on the prowl.

"August was a month of open, merciless fighting, disruption of communications, insecurity for life and property," says one of Hong Kong's most knowledgeable observers of Chinese affairs. "It will be difficult for anyone to impose order."

Only the army holds the country together, some say, and even its position is controversial, its loyalties divided, its efforts to maintain peace half-hearted. Central authority seems to be disintegrating and it appears that the country could sink into the anarchy and lawlessness that marked the early 1900s.

The attempted Cultural Revolution causing all the chaos has long since ceased to be a simple fight over political theories. It has become as difficult to define as to describe. For millions of Chinese, the current upheaval is providing a perfect excuse to settle personal scores, to protest low pay and bad working conditions for the younger people, and to break the monotony of drab lives with travel and excitement.

When Army Wavers

On several occasions, the army has proven its capacity to restore order—if and when given clear instructions and the necessary authority. But conflicting directives from Peking and the fluid nature of the political struggle often have put army commanders in impossible positions, unable to distinguish friend from foe.

One result: Troops have tended to remain on the sidelines, watching various factions fight over which is the most pro-Mao.

Compounding the army's dilemma is an internal split over military doctrine, tied closely to the political storm about ideology versus common sense and professionalism.

At least sixty-five senior army officers already have been removed, including the chief of staff. In China's thirteen major military areas, eight political commissars have been eliminated, and the fate of three others is uncertain. In five of these military areas, possibly more, regional commanders appear to be operating semi-independently of Peking.

One problem for central authorities is that almost all Red Chinese army units have been garrisoned in the same areas since the Korean War. Inevitably, ties have developed with local officials, and vested interests have been created.

Unwillingly, in the meantime, the army has become involved in everything from farm collectives to dockyards. Observers feel that the army presence in such places as factories, mines, power plants and waterworks is mainly symbolic—a visible sign of authority. Principal function of the troops is to maintain order, not production.

A Damaged Image

But this multiplicity of responsibilities, most of them nonmilitary, has damaged the army's image with the public, sapped morale and taken the edge off the combat-readiness of many units which no longer have time for training.

Western military experts, however, warn against downgrading China's overall military capability. In recent years, Peking has given high priority to improving its military establishment. For example, China can produce jet fighter planes. Virtual self-sufficiency has been achieved in petroleum products, including jet fuel.

Fundamentally, the Chinese People's Liberation Army remains a World War II infantry force, but weapons and equipment are far better than those employed in the Korean War. Though China cannot match military might with the United States or Russia, basic needs have been met for what one Western observer calls an army "as good as any in the world at a range of two hundred yards."

Says one Hong Kong authority on Chinese affairs:

"The Chinese could bleed any invader white. And any outside threat could reunify the country to a man."

Military adventures beyond China's borders are more debatable. A fundamental lack of strategic mobility has not been improved by new problems of transport and supply. China's ability to intervene in Vietnam undoubtedly has been whittled down in the last eight months, with the army so involved in civilian affairs. . . .

At the moment, however, direct Chinese participation in the Vietnam war is considered here to be improbable.

Violence to End?

At the moment, there are signs that the Maoist authorities in Peking are trying to turn off the violence as the main harvest season arrives.

One theory held by some Western observers is that Mao Tse-tung is operating on a carefully designed plan of organized confusion. This is the opinion of a US authority on East Asian affairs:

Mao is shaking up his whole country, giving everybody a physical-emotional experience. He takes dead aim on the young—subjecting them to revolutionary experience, complete with violence. Institutions that run the country are the targets in the shake-up. For example:

The Bureaucracy—Mao wants it kept under pressure, and under control of the masses to keep it from being sidetracked from the "continuing revolution."

Education—The system has been put out of action for more than a year. Its goals are being reshaped. Selection of students is to undergo a change.

Officer Corps—Ranks, badges and other trappings of privilege have been eliminated.

The Communist Party—To avoid creating a new class of privileged party functionaries, Mao is getting rid of the handful in authority. Instead of purges and executions, as were the procedures in Russia, Mao accepts repentance from those he seeks to replace.

China Today

Resistance to Mao's objectives is deep and widespread, but unorganized beyond the local level. There has been no open revolt against him. Loyalties and battle lines are so murky that it is misleading to talk or think in terms of civil war.

The key to this Chinese puzzle, in the eyes of Western observers, undoubtedly is in the hands of the army. The possibility is seen of a *coup d'état,* or even a breakup of the Chinese nation into independent or semiautonomous regions ruled by military overlords. Still, China experts feel that, given a choice, military commanders would try for central authority and national unity.

At this time, no end to the chaos and disintegration is discernible. The downward plunge into anarchy has not been arrested, and the near future remains obscure. A major transformation of China seems certainly to lie just ahead.

DECISION OF THE CHINESE COMMUNIST PARTY CENTRAL COMMITTEE CONCERNING THE GREAT CULTURAL REVOLUTION [2]

1. A New Stage of the Socialist Revolution

The current great proletarian Cultural Revolution is a great revolution that touches people to their very souls, representing a more intensive and extensive new stage of the development of Socialist revolution in our country. . . .

[2] From document published in *Survey of the China Mainland Press,* August 16, 1966. Text from *China After Mao,* by A. D. Barnett. Princeton University Press. '67. p 263-76.

Comrade Mao Tse-tung said [that] in order to overthrow a political regime, it is always necessary to prepare the public opinion and carry out work in the ideological field in advance. This is true of the revolutionary class as well as of the counterrevolutionary class. Practice proves that this assertion of Comrade Mao Tse-tung is entirely correct.

Although the bourgeoisie have been overthrown, yet they attempt to use the old ideas, old culture, old customs, and old habits of the exploiting classes to corrupt the mind of man and conquer his heart in a bid to attain the goal of restoring their rule. On the other hand, the proletariat must squarely face all challenges of the bourgeoisie in the ideological sphere, and use its own new ideas, new culture, new customs and new habits to transform the spiritual aspect of the whole society.

At present, our aim is to knock down those power holders who take the capitalist road, criticize the bourgeois reactionary academic "authorities," criticize the ideologies of the bourgeoisie and all exploiting classes, reform education and literature and the arts, and reform all superstructure which is incompatible with the Socialist economic base in order to facilitate the consolidation and development of the Socialist system.

2. The Main Stream and Twists and Turns

The broad masses of workers, peasants and soldiers, revolutionary intellectuals and revolutionary cadres constitute the main force in this great Cultural Revolution. Large numbers of revolutionary youngsters, hitherto unknown, have become brave vanguards. They have energy and wisdom. Using big-character posters and debates, they are airing their views and opinions in a big way, exposing and criticizing in a big way, firmly launching an attack against those open and covert bourgeois representatives. In such a great revolutionary movement, it is inevitable for them to have this or that shortcoming, but their revolutionary direction is right from beginning to end. This is the mainstream of the great proletarian Cultural Revolution. The revolution is continuing its march along this direction.

The Cultural Revolution, being a revolution, will unavoidably meet with resistance, which stems mainly from those power holders who have sneaked into the party and who take the capitalist road. It also comes from the force of old social habits. Such resistance is still rather great and stubborn at present. But the great proletarian Cultural Revolution is a general trend of the time and cannot be resisted. A mass of facts show that if only the masses are fully aroused to action, such resistance will break down quickly.

Owing to the relative great resistance, the struggle may suffer one or several setbacks. Such setbacks will not cause any harm, however. They will only enable the proletarians and other sections of the laboring masses, especially the young ones, to temper themselves, to gain experience and learn lessons, to know that the road of revolution is tortuous and not smooth and straight.

3. The Word "Courage" Must Be Given First Place and the Masses Mobilized With a Free Hand

Whether the leadership of the party dares to mobilize the masses with a free hand will decide the fate of this great Cultural Revolution.

At the moment, party organizations at various levels fall into four categories so far as their leadership of the cultural revolutionary movement is concerned.

1. Some are able to stand in the van of the movement, daring to mobilize the masses with a free hand. Showing "courage," they are Communist fighters who have nothing to fear and good pupils of Chairman Mao. By promoting big-character posters and large-scale debates, they encourage the masses to uncover all demons and monsters, while at the same time encouraging the masses to criticize the shortcomings and mistakes in their work. Such correct leadership stems from the fact that prole-

tarian politics is brought to the fore and the thought of Mao Tse-tung placed in the lead.

2. Responsible officials of many units are still not very clear and not very earnest about their leadership of this great struggle. Providing it with weak leadership, they find themselves in a weak and impotent position. Showing "fear" at every turn, they stick to old rules and regulations, unwilling to break the conventions or seek progress. They are taken by surprise by the revolutionary new order of the masses, with the consequence that their leadership lags behind the situation and the masses.

3. The responsible members of some units make this or that mistake in ordinary times. They are timid and afraid that the masses may pounce on their pigtails [mistakes]. In point of fact, so long as they earnestly conduct self-criticism and accept the criticisms of the masses, they will be forgiven by the party and the masses. Unless they do so, they will continue to make mistakes, thus becoming stumbling blocks to the mass movement.

4. Some units are controlled by power holders who have sneaked into the party and who take the capitalist road. These power holders are extremely afraid that the masses may expose them, and so they find various excuses to suppress the mass movement. Using the tactic of diverting attention from the target and confusing black and white, they attempt to lead the movement astray. When they feel extremely isolated and think that they cannot keep on going their own way, they may execute further plots, shoot at people in the back, manufacture rumors, and do their best to confuse the boundary line between revolution and counterrevolution in order to attack the revolutionaries.

The Party Central Committee requires party committees at various levels to uphold correct leadership, be courageous, mobilize the masses with a free hand, change their state of weakness and impotency, encourage those comrades who have made mistakes but who are willing to make amends to lay down their packs and join the battle, and dismiss the power holders who take the capitalist road, so as to let the leadership return to the hands of proletarian revolutionaries.

4. Let the Masses Educate Themselves in the Movement

In the great proletarian Cultural Revolution, it is the masses who must liberate themselves. We cannot do the things for them which they should do themselves.

We must trust the masses, rely on them, and respect their creative spirit. We must get rid of the word *fear*. We must not be afraid of trouble. Chairman Mao has always told us that revolution is not an elegant, gentle, kind and genial thing. In this great revolutionary movement the masses must be told to educate themselves, to discern what is right and what is wrong, and which ways of doing things are correct and which are incorrect.

Full use must be made of such means as big-character posters and large-scale debates so that views and opinions may be aired and the masses helped to elucidate the correct viewpoints, criticize the erroneous opinions, and uncover all demons and monsters. Only in this way will it be possible to make the broad masses heighten their consciousness in the midst of struggle, increase their capacity for work, and distinguish between the right and wrong and the enemies and ourselves.

5. Party's Class Line Must Be Executed With Resolve

Who is our enemy and who is our friend? This question is a primary question of the revolution, as well as a primary question of the Cultural Revolution.

The party leadership must be good at discovering the leftists, developing and expanding the ranks of the leftists, and resolutely relying on the revolutionary leftists. Only in this way can we in the movement completely isolate the mass of reactionary rightists, win over the middle-of-the-roaders, and rally the great majority. Through the movement we shall then ultimately unite with over 95 percent of the cadres and with over 95 percent of the masses.

Forces should be concentrated on attacking a handful of extremely reactionary bourgeois rightists and counterrevolutionary revisionists. Their antiparty, anti-Socialist, and anti-thought-of-Mao-Tse-tung crimes must be fully exposed and criticized, and they must be isolated to the maximum extent.

The focus of this movement is on the purge of those power holders within the party who take the capitalist road.

A strict distinction must be drawn between the antiparty and anti-Socialist rightists and those who support the party and socialism but who have made some wrong remarks, done some wrong things, or written some bad articles or books.

A strict distinction must also be drawn between the bourgeois reactionary scholar-tyrants and reactionary "authorities" and people who hold bourgeois academic ideas of a general nature.

6. Contradictions Among the People Must Be Correctly Handled

It is necessary to strictly separate the two kinds of contradictions of different character—those among the people and those between the enemy and ourselves. Contradictions among the people must not be treated as contradictions between the enemy and ourselves or the other way round.

That differing opinions are found among the people is a normal phenomenon. Controversy between various kinds of opinion is not only unavoidable but necessary and beneficial. In the course of normal and unreserved debates the masses are capable of affirming what is correct and rectifying what is wrong, and gradually attaining unanimity.

In the course of debate, it is essential to adopt the method of putting facts on the table, explaining the reasons, and convincing people with truth. To the minority of people who hold different opinions the method of suppression must not be applied. The minority must be protected because sometimes truth is in the hand of the minority. Even if the opinions of the minority were wrong, they should be permitted to put forward their arguments and to reserve their own opinions.

In the course of the debates, people may argue with one another but must not use their fists.

In the course of debate, every revolutionary must be good at independent thinking, promoting the Communist spirit of daring to think, speak, and act. Under the premise of a direction, a revolutionary comrade should not argue endlessly on questions of technicalities in order to strengthen solidarity.

7. Be Alert Against Those Who Label Revolutionary Masses as "Counterrevolutionaries"

In some schools, some units and some work teams, responsible members have organized a counterattack against the masses who posted big-character wall-newspapers against them. They even intimated that to oppose the leaders of their own units or work teams was to oppose the Party Central Committee, the party and socialism, and that any slogan shouted in this regard was a counterrevolutionary slogan. By so doing they will necessarily attack some real revolutionary activists. This is a wrong direction to take and a wrong line to follow. It is impermissible to do so.

Some who are seriously affected by erroneous thinking, and even some antiparty and anti-Socialist rightists, make use of certain shortcomings and mistakes in the mass movement to spread rumors and carry out instigations, purposely representing some masses as counterrevolutionaries. We must beware of such "pickpockets," and expose their tricks in time.

In the movement, with the exception of existing counterrevolutionaries who have been proved to have committed murders, arson, poison spreading, sabotage and stealing of state secrets and who should be dealt with in accordance with law, problems among students of universities, specialized colleges, middle schools and primary schools should not lead to their purge. In order to prevent the shifting of the main target of struggle, it is impermissible to use any excuse to instigate the masses to struggle against the masses and students to struggle against students. Even in the case of real rightists, they should be dealt with in the light of prevailing circumstances at a late period in the movement.

8. The Cadre Question

Cadres may generally be classified into four types:

1. The good
2. The relatively good
3. Those with serious mistakes but who are not antiparty and anti-Socialist elements
4. A small number of antiparty and anti-Socialist rightists

Under general conditions, the first two types of cadres (the good and the relatively good) are in the majority.

Antiparty and anti-Socialist rightists must be fully exposed and knocked down, their influence must be eliminated and at the same time they should be given a chance to start anew.

9. Cultural Revolutionary Groups, Cultural Revolutionary Committees, and Cultural Revolutionary Congresses

In the course of the great proletarian Cultural Revolution, many new things have begun to appear. In many schools and units, such organizational forms as cultural revolutionary groups and cultural revolutionary committees created by the masses are new things of great historic significance.

Cultural revolutionary groups, cultural revolutionary committees and cultural revolutionary congresses are the best new organizational forms for the self-education of the masses under the leadership of the Communist party. They are the best bridges for strengthening the contact between the party and the masses. They are power organs of the proletarian Cultural Revolution.

The struggle of the proletariat against old ideas, old culture, old customs and old habits left over from all exploiting classes for the past thousands of years will take a very long time. In view of this, cultural revolutionary groups, cultural revolutionary committees, and cultural revolutionary congresses should not be temporary organizations but should be permanent mass organizations. They are applicable not only to schools and organs but basically also to industrial and mining enterprises, streets and the countryside.

Members of the cultural revolutionary groups and cultural revolutionary committees and delegates to the cultural revolutionary congresses must be fully elected as in the Paris Commune. The name list of the candidates must be drawn up and submitted by the revolutionary masses, and after repeated discussions by the masses elections may then be held.

Members of the cultural revolutionary groups and cultural revolutionary committees and delegates to the cultural revolutionary congresses may be criticized by the masses at any time and, if they are found to be derelict in their duties, may be replaced by election after discussion by the masses.

In schools, cultural revolutionary groups, cultural revolutionary committees and cultural revolutionary congresses should take revolutionary students as the mainstay. At the same time, a certain number of revolutionary teachers and staff members should participate in them.

10. Teaching Reform

Reforming the old educational system and the old policy and method of teaching is an extremely vital task of the great proletarian Cultural Revolution.

In this great Cultural Revolution, it is necessary to completely change the situation where our schools are dominated by bourgeois intellectuals.

In schools of all types, it is imperative to carry out the policy, advanced by Comrade Mao Tse-tung, of making education serve proletarian politics and having education integrated with productive labor, so that those who get an education may develop morally, intellectually and physically and become Socialist-minded, cultured laborers.

The academic course must be shortened and the curricula simplified. Teaching materials must be thoroughly reformed, and the more complex material must be simplified first of all. Students should take as their main task the study of their proper courses and also learn other things. Besides studying academic subjects, they should also learn to do industrial, agricultural and military work. They must also be prepared to participate in the cultural revolutionary struggle for criticizing the bourgeoisie.

11. The Question of Criticism by Name in the Press

In carrying out the cultural revolutionary mass movement, it is essential to combine the dissemination of the proletarian world outlook, Marxism-Leninism and the thought of Mao Tse-tung with the criticism of the bourgeois and feudal ideologies.

It is necessary to organize criticism of those bourgeois representatives who have wormed their way into the party and the bourgeois reactionary academic "authorities," including the criticism of various reactionary viewpoints on all fronts of philosophy, history, political economy, education, literature and art, literary and art theory, and theory of natural sciences.

Criticism by name in the press must first be discussed by the party committees at the corresponding levels, and in some cases approved by the higher party committees.

12. Policy Toward Scientists, Technicians, and Working Personnel in General

Toward scientists, technicians and [scientific and technical] working personnel in general, provided that they love their country, work actively, are not against the party and socialism, and do not secretly collaborate with any foreign power(s) the policy of unity-criticism-unity should continue to be adopted in this movement. Scientists and scientific and technical personnel who have made valuable contributions should be protected. They may be assisted in gradually transforming their world outlook and styles of work.

13. The Question of Arrangements for Combining [the Cultural Revolution] Education Movement in Town and Countryside

In big and medium cities cultural and educational units and party and government leadership organs are the key points of the present proletarian Cultural Revolution.

The great Cultural Revolution has made the Socialist education movement in town and countryside even richer in content and better. It is necessary to combine the two. Arrangements to this end may be worked out by various localities and departments in the light of actual conditions.

In the countryside and in urban enterprises where the Socialist education movement is carried out, if the original arrangements are suitable and are properly carried out, they should not be disturbed, and work should continue in accordance with the original arrangements. However, questions raised by the present proletarian Cultural Revolution movement must in a suitable moment be handed over to the masses for discussion so that the proletarian ideology may be made to flourish and the bourgeois ideology destroyed.

In some places, with the proletarian Cultural Revolution as the center, the Socialist education movement is led forward, and one's politics, thinking, relations with one's organization and economic circumstances are made clear. Such practices may be permitted where the party committee considers them proper.

14. Grasp the Revolution and Promote Production

The great proletarian Cultural Revolution is aimed at enabling man to revolutionize his thinking and consequently enabling work in all fields to be done with greater, faster, better and more economical results. Provided the masses are fully mobilized and satisfactory arrangements are made, it is possible to guarantee that the Cultural Revolution and production will not impede each other and that a high quality of work in all fields will be attained.

The great proletarian Cultural Revolution is a mighty motive force for developing our country's social productivity. It is wrong to set the great Cultural Revolution against the development of production.

15. The Army

The cultural revolutionary movement and the Socialist education movement in the armed forces should be conducted in accordance with the directives of the Military Commission of the Party Central Committee and the General Political Department of the PLA [People's Liberation Army].

16. The Thought of Mao Tse-tung Is the Guide for the Proletarian Cultural Revolution

In the course of the great proletarian Cultural Revolution, it is necessary to hold high the great Red banner of the thought of Mao Tse-tung and to place proletarian politics in command. The movement for creatively studying and applying Chairman Mao's works must be launched among the broad masses of workers, peasants and soldiers, cadres and intellectuals. The thought of Mao Tse-tung must be regarded as a compass to the Cultural Revolution. . . .

Party committees at various levels must abide by the successive directives of Chairman Mao, implement the mass line of coming from the masses and returning to the masses, and be pupils first and teachers later. They must make an effort to avoid one-sidedness and limitations. They must promote materialistic dialectics and oppose metaphysics and scholasticism.

Under the leadership of the party center headed by Comrade Mao Tse-tung, the great proletarian Cultural Revolution will surely win a grand victory.

THE CULTURAL REVOLUTION:
ITS ZIGS AND ZAGS [3]

For a long time the nation has not been satisfied with you. All officials, in and out of the capital, know that your mind is not right, that you are too arbitrary, that you are perverse. You think that you alone are right, you refuse to accept criticism and your mistakes are many.—Excerpt from a 1961 play, *Hai Jui Dismissal from Office,* by Wu Han.

An attack on Wu Han's play about the Ming dynasty is now widely regarded as the opening shot of Communist China's "great proletarian Cultural Revolution" of 1966-67. In November 1965 a Shanghai newspaper attacked the play, calling it a poisonous weed and accusing author Wu Han (Peking's deputy mayor, leading historian, and university professor) of using "the past to ridicule the present." The newspaper claimed that Wu Han's criticism of the emperor was intended for none other than China's venerable leader Mao Tse-tung.

This initial signal of the turmoil to come went almost unnoticed by the outside world. But later Western observers noted that the first newspaper attacks on Wu Han coincided with Mao's mysterious disappearance, which lasted from November 1965 to May 1966. According to some, Mao spent the five months in Shanghai plotting a campaign against leading party officials; according to others, he was recovering from a serious illness. Mao reappeared a month after the public launching of the Cultural Revolution. . . .

The opening campaign centered on Peking where Mayor P'eng Chen, a senior Politburo member and a deputy director of the party's propaganda department, made his last appearance in late March 1966. The Peking Municipal Committee of the party which P'eng headed was attacked as an "independent kingdom, water-tight and impenetrable and nobody was allowed to intervene or criticize it—it was like a tiger whose backside no one dared to kick."

[3] From *Facts and Issues*. League of Women Voters. 1730 M St. N.W. Washington, D.C. 20036. '68. p 1-2. Reprinted by permission.

Focusing on China's literary and art circles as well as the educational system (especially the universities which Mao regarded as a breeding ground for dissidence), the campaign soon surpassed in intensity the party's previous rectification campaigns. By August 1966, more than 195 prominent cultural figures had been removed from their positions. Educators, journalists, writers, artists, composers, publishers, and the regime's entire party propaganda apparatus were all held responsible for the "disease of bourgeois ideology." It became increasingly apparent to China watchers that Mao was attempting to flush out dissidence, both in and outside the party, which had been rife during the 1961-62 liberalization (a milder version of the 1956 Hundred Flowers Movement when China's intellectuals had given full vent to their criticisms). It was during the 1961 period that intellectuals resorted to allegory to express their disaffection with policies of the 1958 Great Leap Forward.

The second stage of the Cultural Revolution—emphasizing rectification of the party—began on August 18, 1966, when Lin Piao emerged as Mao's heir apparent (replacing President Liu Shao-ch'i, who was No. 2 man in the party for thirty years). [Former Defense Minister Lin Piao was reportedly killed in a plane crash in 1971 while trying to flee the country after planning to assassinate Mao and seize control of the government.—Ed.] On the same day, Mao also launched the newly created Red Guards.

In addition, Mao called upon the People's Liberation Army (PLA) to serve as a revolutionary model for the whole country. From its inception, the PLA had been used as an indoctrination school, and Mao relied increasingly on Lin Piao and the PLA's General Political Department to inject new energy into the revolution and to educate the next generation for continued struggle. In fact, the famous little red book of Mao's sayings was first produced for the army in 1961.

With the support of the PLA, Mao organized the Red Guards as a shock force to "boldly arouse the masses." Also, of course, Mao hoped to heighten the teenagers' revolutionary fervor. A Red Guard vanguard, created in June 1966 from a middle school attached to Tsinghua University in Peking, served as a model. Many guards came from middle schools and colleges which Mao had ordered closed. They were recruited primarily in terms of militancy and revolutionary zeal and restricted to five "Red classes—workers, poor and lower-class peasants and revolutionary cadres, and revolutionary martyrs."

The rampage of the Red Guards began in August 1966. Setting out to destroy the four "olds" (old ideas, old culture, old customs, and old habits), they covered Peking with posters stating that all bourgeois remnants must be destroyed. Day-by-day destruction and violence mounted. Street signs with Western names were torn down, religious monuments destroyed, private homes entered, and jewelry, antiques, and other bourgeois possessions burned or confiscated. Red Guard disorders soon spread from Peking to Shanghai, Canton, and other urban centers.

Between August and September, over 10 million of some 150 million teenagers in China appeared at nine mass rallies in Peking where they viewed their great leader—Chairman Mao. Such mass meetings made it possible to bypass the conventional party apparatus.

Simultaneously conducting a campaign within the party machinery controlled by Liu Shao-ch'i, Mao formed his own extraparty organization and channels of communication. The most important organ created by Mao was the Cultural Revolutionary Group headed by Ch'en Po-ta, formerly his political secretary. Lin Piao and Chiang Ching, Mao's actress wife, also had top roles on the new team. Old comrades and high-ranking cadres were principal targets of this rectification-purge campaign.

The attack centered more and more on Liu Shao-ch'i and the alliances which his faction had apparently developed throughout China. In December 1966, Mao began a campaign to discredit Liu. He was labeled China's Khrushchev in the spring of 1967. Liu was condemned as the "pragmatist" who had assumed control after the crop disasters of the early 1960s and modified the commune system by granting small private plots to peasants and instigating other capitalistic practices.

Chou En-lai, prime minister and No. 3 man in the party, is the only leader left who has occupied an important position in the Chinese Communist party from its inception. Left unscathed by various leadership changes, Chou is known to the Chinese as Bu Tou-wong, a name for a child's weighted doll that always bounces back to its original position. While going along with Mao and Lin Piao in the power struggle, he acts increasingly as a moderating influence to prevent the total paralysis of his administrative units and the complete breakdown between Peking and recalcitrant provinces.

The Cultural Revolution continued to zig and zag. Months of turmoil came to a climax in December 1966 and January 1967 when chaos apparently spread over much of China. Remote provinces, as well as major cities, were involved in the struggle. China watchers started speculating as to whether the central government still maintained control. The Red Guards extended their activities to the factories. Rival groups contended for power—"revolutionaries" vs. "those taking the capitalist road." Recurring periods of great disorder took place in May and again in July 1967, with the army directed to restore order with each new wave of disorder. One of the more violent events was an uprising in the Yangtze River city of Wuhan, which resulted in the kidnapping and beating of two of Mao's top aides, who had to be rescued by Chou En-lai.

By August another slogan was issued: "Support the army and cherish the people." Instructions emphasized "unity" and "alliances" between rebel groups, party cadres, and the military. All "wayward" cadres, except the most incorrigible, were exhorted to make amends and return to the side of Chairman Mao. Attempts were made to get the Red Guards back in school although only a few schools apparently . . . reopened.

In late October thousands of army troops were sent to the countryside to propagate Mao's policies on agriculture and to help bring in the harvest. Red Guard and other pro-Mao elements throughout the country were told to stop "armed struggle" among themselves and to form "revolutionary alliances" with repentant cadres.

There is no way to assess from afar the effect of the Cultural Revolution on the pattern of life in Communist China. Obviously education has been affected and intellectual life restricted. The family may have been disrupted by the activities of the Red Guards. It is not clear whether the economy has been seriously damaged. However, reports have described transportation stoppages, refusals of peasants to turn over autumn bumper crops, industrial shutdowns, and disruption of overseas shipping.

What are the dynamics underlying the current struggle? Is the Cultural Revolution primarily Mao's attempt to revitalize revolutionary fervor? To cement the second generation to communism? To combat rising forces of politically alienated "revisionists?" To restrain nonideological managerial and scientific forces? The answers probably lie in a complexity of interacting factors.

Many observers say the Cultural Revolution is drawing to an end. Others counsel that the revolutionary process is, in Mao's words, "like waves of the sea," with an inevitable succession of alternating periods of calm and turbulence.

A NATION IN AGONY [4]

The most startling news from Communist China in recent months has been the frenzied rampage of young people calling themselves the "Red Guards of the Cultural Revolution." Obviously the Red Guards have mounted their cam-

[4] From article by Theodore Hsi-en Chen, director, East Asian Studies Center, University of California. *Problems of Communism* (U.S. Information Agency). 15:14-20. N./D. '66.

paign with official instigation and approval. The big question is: what are the Chinese Communists up to? Why are they indulging in destructive acts that risk nullifying the gains they have made in the past seventeen years of Communist rule?

No one can deny that the Communists have accomplished much since the birth of their regime. Politically, they have forged an intricate system of government and party administration that exercises effective authority in all parts of mainland China. Economically, they have made a good start towards industrialization, and the more rational policies pursued since the collapse of the Great Leap have brought a revival of agriculture and a better economic balance. The growth of state revenues and domestic stability have enabled the government to project its influence abroad and to extend aid to Asian and African countries. In the area of social reform, the Communists have substantially reduced social and economic inequality and established greatly expanded public welfare services; they have established an extensive system of full-time and part-time schools, for adults as well as school-age students, so that there are more educational institutions and more students enrolled in them than at any previous time in China's history. In view of all this, it is not surprising that many visitors to the Chinese mainland have come away highly impressed by the achievements of what appears to be a dynamic society under the leadership of an efficient and energetic, if rigidly totalitarian, government.

Significant as these achievements are, however, they represent only a part of the Chinese Communist program of revolution. The Communists are not satisfied with building a strong and prosperous China; they must push ahead to establish a new society and a new way of life. For them, it is not enough to have a government exercising effective control, not enough to have a stable and growing economy, not enough to have the piecemeal social reforms that are customarily sought by bourgeois-liberal reformers. Such developments are desirable only insofar as they constitute an advance toward the ultimate goal of establishing socialism and communism. Communism calls for the establishment of a new society, not only with new institutions but also with new social and economic relationships reflecting a new ideology, and with new loyalties and new attitudes to reinforce the ideology. It demands no less than a new type of man for a new social order. It requires fundamental changes in the minds and hearts of the people.

The "great proletarian Cultural Revolution" that has been gradually gathering momentum in mainland China since 1965 and has produced the Red Guards of 1966 is in essence a redoubled effort to change the minds and hearts of China's millions. This is not the first time that such an effort has been made. It is precisely because the previous attempts were not altogether successful that a massive new campaign has been deemed necessary by the Communist regime.

The Communists were reaching a peak of achievement and confidence in 1957. . . . Premier Chou En-lai noted with satisfaction the success of the new regime in consolidating its power. Five major campaigns, he said, had helped to achieve this consolidation. They were: (1) the agrarian land reform campaign to destroy feudalism and the landlord class; (2) the "Resist-America, Aid-Korea" campaign to combat American "imperialism" and root out its evil influences in Chinese society; (3) the drive against "counterrevolutionaries" to eliminate opposition; (4) the "three-anti" and "five-anti" campaigns directed at the urban bourgeoisie; and (5) the ideological remolding movement designed to change the outlook, thought patterns, and basic loyalties of the whole people, especially the intellectuals.

These campaigns all took place in the early years of the regime. It should also be noted that although ideological remolding is listed as a separate campaign, it was actually involved in every one of the other four. One of the essential purposes of the agrarian reform was to instill "class consciousness" in the peasants and teach them to wage bitter class struggle against the landlords. The "Resist-America" drive, though linked directly with the Korean War, had the broader aim of eliminating ideas and attitudes traceable to American influence. The targets of the campaign against "counterrevolutionaries" were not strictly limited to those who committed outright acts of opposition against the new regime; they included those whose thinking was not in line with the new ideology. And the campaign directed at the urban bourgeoisie sought to combat "bourgeois ideology" and the "bourgeois way of life" as well as to suppress capitalism in economic life.

From the beginning of their regime, therefore, the Communists have stressed the supreme importance of changing the minds and hearts of the people. But this has proven to be an extremely difficult task. It was relatively easy to divest the landlords of their property and influence, even to liquidate a good many of them. It was a simple task to take over the educational institutions supported by American funds and cleanse the school curriculum of American-influenced subjects of study. The "counterrevolutionaries" were quickly silenced and the bourgeoisie compelled to submit to the new regulations for industry and commerce. But "unproletarian" ideas still persisted. After a decade and a half punctuated by successive campaigns of "ideological remolding" and "thought reform," the Communists came to the disconcerting realization that their battle for the minds and hearts of China's millions had not made much headway. The intellectuals still harbored bourgeois ideas, and the people were still moved by desires and ambitions unworthy of a collective Socialist society.

Mao's regime came to power in 1949. During the first few months, the Communists pursued a policy of relative moderation in order to allay the fears of the population. They talked about New Democracy instead of socialism and communism, implying that no drastic changes were impending.

After the Korean War, their major concern was the consolidation of power. The agrarian reform put the rural population under their control. The suppression of "counterrevolutionaries" eliminated political opposition. The class struggles against landlords and the urban bourgeoisie strengthened the position of "proletarian leadership." Anti-American agitation and ideological remolding attacked potential sources of resistance to the Communist ideology.

The consolidation of power, in essence a political revolution, paved the way for the economic revolution—the first Five-Year Plan (1953-57) and the transition to socialism. The New Democracy was terminated, and the era of socialism began in 1954. "A new upsurge in the Socialist mass movement" was declared to be in progress, agriculture was collectivized, and private industry and commerce were "transformed" into Socialist enterprises. These were the years in which the Communist regime's positive achievements in economic rehabilitation and material construction won widespread recognition abroad. But for the Chinese Communists, who could not be satisfied with anything less than a total revolution embracing every phase of individual and group life, there was still something lacking. Beneath the outward submission and the conformity, the people still clung to ideas, thoughts, and attitudes which were basically inimical to the political, economic and social collectivism which the Communists considered essential to their new society. There was the danger that these old ideas, thoughts, habits, attitudes—the "old" way of life, in short—might reassert themselves and jeopardize the visible, surface gains that had been made. It was this danger that the Communists had in mind when they issued frequent warnings against a possible "rebirth of capitalism" and a revival of bourgeois ideology.

While the Communists were hitherto concerned with concrete tasks of political and economic transformation, with the tangible process of replacing old institutions with new ones, the Cultural Revolution has less specific targets. It is aimed at the minds and hearts of the people and what goes on in them under the cover of apparent conformity—at sentiments and habits of thought which, the Communists fear, could reassert themselves and become the wellspring of re-

sistance and opposition, even open rebellion. The fact that
the Chinese Communist leaders still today speak out against
those who hope for a "Hungarian uprising" [i.e., armed re-
bellion] in China shows that they do not discount even
this extreme possibility.

The need for getting at the mainspring of the revolution
—the minds and hearts of the people—has become more
pressing in recent years. While due credit for the substantial
achievements of the middle 1950s must be given to the Communists' organizational ability and the stimulus imparted
by an energetic government, a major factor contributing to
those successes was the initial enthusiastic response of the
public to the new regime's appeal for hard work and con-
certed action to build a strong nation. Having yearned so
long for a return to peace that would give them the opportunity to make long-range plans and exercise their frustrated
capabilities, the Chinese people eagerly responded to the
Communists' catchy slogans and patriotic appeals. They put
forth their best efforts and made possible the production
records that distinguished the first Five-Year Plan. The second Five-Year Plan (1957-62) was inaugurated with fanfare
and extravagant promises, but these promises were not fulfilled. Instead, thanks to the ill-conceived and impetuous
policies of the Great Leap Forward and the communes, serious economic dislocations became evident before the end of
1959, and the country was plunged into an economic crisis
in 1960-62 that caused widespread suffering and disillusion-
ment and drove large numbers of refugees across the border
into Hong Kong. Natural disasters and the withdrawal of
Soviet aid helped to aggravate the crisis, to be sure, but a
major factor in the collapse was the fact that the people lost
the enthusiasm and motivation of the earlier years. The acceleration of collectivism, the establishment of the communes
with their public mess halls and public nurseries, the encroachments on personal and family life, threatened to deprive the people of things that they held particularly dear
and precious. Having worked hard and given up much, they

began to wonder whether they would ever enjoy the fruits of their labor. They slackened their effort, and production declined. The morale of the nation dropped to a low level.

The economic collapse of 1960-62 forced the Communists to take a few grudging steps backward. Bowing to practical necessity, they permitted the peasants to cultivate small private plots, raise livestock, and market their own produce, and they sought to revive industrial activity by providing material incentives for the workers. These concessions succeeded in effecting a substantial measure of economic recovery, but the Communists found it difficult to rekindle the enthusiasm and optimism of the earlier years. The major problem confronting them has not been one of devising additional governmental machinery or designing new economic institutions, but rather one of dealing with the people's state of mind, of reviving the élan and patriotic zeal that characterized the early 1950s. The challenge to the Communists today, therefore, is not primarily economic or political in the narrow sense, but psychological and cultural. The term "Cultural Revolution" accurately reflects the nature of the problem.

Besides internal factors, the Sino-Soviet dispute has had considerable impact on the public state of mind. For years after coming to power, the new regime carried on a massive nationwide campaign to promote a feeling of brotherhood toward the USSR. The whole nation was instructed to "learn from the Soviet Union," and friendship with the USSR was written into the Chinese Communist constitution as a cardinal principle. In 1960, however, the official line was abruptly reversed. The nation was now told that the Soviet leaders were betraying the proletarian cause. The very people who had been affectionately called Big Brothers were now reviled as "enemies" of the revolution. This complete about-face must have confused the people. They could hardly help but wonder if the "truths" taught by Communist propaganda and indoctrination were reliable, and whether other "truths" besides "undying friendship" with the USSR might not prove equally false. Once the people begin to question the veracity of Communist propaganda, a major pillar of the Communist edifice becomes weakened. Here, again, the problem is one of dealing with mental attitudes, with motivations and morale. These are matters of the mind and heart.

It is not merely coincidental that the Cultural Revolution has taken its heaviest toll among those whose activities most directly influence people's minds. A significantly large proportion of those singled out for virulent attack have been novelists, playwrights, poets, filmmakers, historians, newspaper editors, and university professors—i.e., people who work in the realm of ideas and who communicate their ideas to others. Communist officials responsible for propaganda, indoctrination, and implementation of the party's cultural policies have also been attacked.

One of the chief targets of the Cultural Revolution has been "revisionism." By this is meant not only the Khrushchev brand of communism but any ideas at variance with the orthodox Chinese Communist party line. The reason why the current campaign has swelled to such vast proportions is that the Communist leadership now recognizes that revisionism exists not just in a few isolated pockets of the population, but virtually everywhere in China. Its roots are in the minds and hearts of citizens who do not and will not easily relinquish the values, ideas, habits, sentiments, ambitions, and loyalties they have inherited from the past. Some of the major sources of revisionism may be briefly identified.

First, there are many patriotic Chinese who are moved by nationalism, but not by communism. They want to do all they can to help rid China of all traces of foreign domination and build a strong and independent nation, but they have no enthusiasm for any ideology or political party as such. They do not make good partisans.

Second, there are liberals who from an early date warmly supported the Communists' proposals for reform because they themselves were deeply dissatisfied with the old social order. They are, however, not committed to the ideology the Communists consider essential to their program. Furthermore, the Communists attack "reformism" and "reformers" as incompatible with their stress on "revolution" and "revolutionaries." To advocate gradual reform or partial change is, in the Communist view, to be guilty of revisionism.

Third, the masses want better living conditions and a better livelihood, and they want these things right now, or at least in the foreseeable future. These aspirations, however, run counter to Communist preachments of disciplined living, acceptance of hardships, toughness of character, and sacrifice of personal comfort and welfare.

Fourth, many people in China do not subscribe to the Marxist theory of class and class struggle. Indeed, the latter concept is totally alien to traditional Confucian philosophy with its emphasis on social harmony. To the doctrinaire Communist, however, class consciousness is the very essence and prerequisite of a revolutionary outlook.

Fifth, the intellectuals do not readily fall into line. Even though they may outwardly submit to the party's demands for ideological conformity and thought reform, they have tended, at times of relaxed official controls, to reassert their independence and even to give veiled expression to bourgeois or antiproletarian ideas.

Sixth, traditional social and cultural values persist despite strong official condemnation. Among them are attachment to home and family; aversion to collective life and to soldiery; reverence for Confucianism and its way of life; long-established social customs reinforced by deep sentiments; etc. These attitudes and values resist change and stand in the way of the total political and social transformation that the Communists seek to carry through. The Cultural Revolution of 1965-66 is, in large part, a frenzied all-out effort to stamp out these entrenched traditions of the old society.

Seventh, technologists and professional people resent political interference with their activities. They do not accept the Communist principle of letting politics take command. They place technology and professional competence above political and ideological orthodoxy. They include educators who want to put more emphasis on academic learning, technical personnel who feel that Marxism-Leninism and the thought of Mao Tse-tung cannot take the place of technical expertise, and even military leaders who are more concerned with building a strong modern army than with political indoctrination or using soldiers for "productive labor."

Eighth, even among the Communists themselves, there is now a younger generation which has not experienced the bitter struggle that characterized the early years of the Communist movement in China, and which consequently does not share the fiery and single-minded dedication of the veterans.

Ninth, there are also Communists who would like to see the leadership adopt more moderate and realistic policies. They are afraid that the present hard, dogmatic approach will alienate public support and undermine the Communist regime. They urge, among other things, less haste in collectivization and more attention to the practical tasks of building a strong nation and a healthy economy.

Tenth, there is always the danger that the Socialist changes effected by the regime may be gradually weakened and ultimately nullified by a "rebirth of capitalism." Private plots for the peasants, material incentives for labor, concessions to the remaining Chinese ex-capitalists—all of these pose a continuing threat to socialism and collectivism.

More might be added to the list. What the doctrinaire Communists call revisionism is likely to rear its head from many sections of the population and from varied areas of national life. The antirevisionist campaign, therefore, must necessarily be long in duration and pervasive in scope.

The task of changing the minds and hearts of the people is fundamentally one of education, indoctrination, and propaganda, which are practically synonymous terms in the Communist lexicon. A cardinal principle of Chinese Communist education is that it must serve proletarian politics. In other words, its first duty is to propagate and implant Communist ideology and ideas; it must produce a new type of man with a new mind and new loyalties. This task is undertaken on at least three basic levels.

First, the thoughts and motivations of the masses at large must be remolded. Academic instruction is only a secondary aspect of mass education in Communist China. The more important objective of Communist indoctrination is to teach the people to love collective life, to work for the common good as defined by the party-state, and to be willing to sacrifice material benefits and present comfort for the long-range success of the revolution.

A second level of the educational effort is directed specifically at the youth of the nation. It is from the younger generation that the regime has drawn the activists and cadres who are now the backbone of the Chinese Communist movement. From their ranks must come the "successors" who will take over the leadership from the now aging veterans of the Communist revolution. They must be taught Communist morality. In them must be instilled a fiery and unflagging devotion to the revolution.

Thirdly, there is the crucial and most vexing problem of the intellectuals. Despite successive campaigns of "thought reform," many of them remain unconverted to communism. They have made the required public confessions and pledges of "heart surrender," but, whenever the regime's controls are slightly relaxed, their unproletarian ideas find expression in one form or another. They may conform in action, or even pay apparent homage to the regime, but their minds and hearts seem to be basically unchanged. They must be won over, however, if the revolution is to succeed. Their services are badly needed, and their traditional position in society enables them to exert great influence.

The events of 1960-62 seem to have convinced the Chinese Communist leaders that the program of education and indoctrination needed to be greatly intensified. Accordingly, a campaign of Socialist education was launched with the broad purpose of rekindling revolutionary fervor and impressing upon the people the necessity of waging a bitter and unremitting class struggle against all unproletarian persons and ideas. Reporting to the National People's Congress in December 1964, Premier Chou En-lai already applied to this mounting campaign the name of Cultural Revolution. "It is necessary," he declared, "to bring about a radical transformation of all bourgeois, feudal, and other forms of ideology and culture which are not suited to the Socialist economic base and political system, and to carry forward the Socialist revolution on the ideological and cultural fronts to the end."

The great proletarian Cultural Revolution of 1966, therefore, is not a sudden development, but simply a new and more violent phase of the continuing battle the Communists are waging for the minds and hearts of China's millions. It is a desperate and frenzied effort to achieve what more than a decade and a half of ideological remolding has —by admission of the Chinese Communists themselves— failed to accomplish.

III. HOW THE CHINESE LIVE AND WORK

EDITOR'S INTRODUCTION

In the mass of conflicting and sometimes ambiguous data now coming from mainland China, there seems to be general agreement on a number of points. Among these points are the following: that living conditions have improved noticeably over the last two decades, though China is still an extremely poor country both in terms of its own goals and even more so relative to Western standards; that most people seem to work long hours for relatively low pay, but that they appear to be adequately, if simply, fed, housed, and clothed; that while consumer goods are available in the cities in increasing amounts, they are often prohibitively expensive in terms of salary; that there has been a great cleanup in the cities and many of the formerly infamous slums have been improved or eliminated; that there is what by Western standards would be an intolerable amount of regimentation in the society, but that many people are enthusiastic about serving the state and helping it reach its goals.

The first article in this section is written by a journalist who had lived in China for ten years prior to 1949 and returned in 1972 when President Nixon visited China. The author offers a knowledgeable and informative account of China today. He notes the many changes which have occurred and concludes that life seems to be earnest—and rather grim. The next article, from *Time,* describes aspects of daily life and then goes on to draw a picture of the peasant, the worker, and the soldier in China today.

The third article, from the *Wall Street Journal,* examines how industry functions. The author notes that for each individual factory self-reliance seems to be the watchword. Among other things, this means that China is consciously making an effort to exclude dependence on imported supplies. In part, this reflects China's rather isolated position in world affairs.

The next piece is by a former United Nations official who has made numerous trips to China. He notes the progress made by China in a number of areas in the 1950s and 1960s. The last article in the section speaks of what it is like to live and work on a Chinese agricultural commune.

This selection of articles, though it does not cover all aspects of the economy, offers a representative sample of living and working conditions in China. No doubt, in some areas conditions are much more difficult than those here described. However, the general impression is that economically China is on the move after dismal decades of stagnation.

CHINA REVISITED [1]

Reprinted from *U.S. News & World Report.*

This is a report about a China that really exists, not a China of the imagination or one created by propaganda. That part of the country I have just seen is healthier, more prosperous, and far more orderly than the China I left in 1949 after the Communists had seized the mainland.

The people I saw and talked with are better fed, better dressed, bigger and huskier than the generation that had fought—or sat out—eight years of Japanese occupation and four years of brutal civil war.

Medical services are incomparably improved and reach far more families than ever before. In the countryside and in the cities, housing is better, though far below US standards. Food supplies seem to be satisfactory, at least in the cities I visited, and consumer goods—most of them utilitarian, although you do see toys and decorative items for the home—are available. A Chinese cannot buy an automobile or a TV set for his personal use, and most of the sewing machines I

[1] From article by Robert P. Martin, directing editor, international staff. *U.S. News & World Report.* 72:22-6+. Mr. 13, '72.

saw offered for sale at the equivalent of $75 were operated by foot pedal, not by electricity.

The "luxuries" which some Chinese can afford to buy are wristwatches, transistor radios and bicycles. Since the latter are used to go to and from work, they are priced relatively low by Chinese standards: $75 to $90. None that I saw had multiple-speed shifts. Other "luxuries" are quite expensive, even by US standards.

The stores I visited in Peking, Hangchow and Shanghai during President Nixon's trip to mainland China are amply supplied with consumer goods, and people seem to have some money to spend. I was told that a working family—mother and father—can save from $12 to $14 a month.

The products are almost all made in Chinese factories. Foreign-made goods, aside from what is needed by industry and agriculture, are almost nonexistent.

Costly Gains

The Chinese, as an individual, seems to me to have paid a rather heavy price for these economic gains. His life is regimented.

The government tells him where he can work, and he can be—and often is—sent to work in factories or on communes far from his home and family.

The newspaper he reads or the news programs he hears on the radio are not controversial, not even very informative. He has access only to what the government wants him to know.

There are no policy options which he and his friends can debate or discuss except in times of great turmoil, such as during the Cultural Revolution.

Young people, I was told, are permitted to enroll in schools of higher education only if they are the children of peasants, workers or soldiers, and they must be "recommended" by the all-powerful "revolutionary committee" of their communes or factories.

Most of the people I saw in the cities seemed docile or indifferent. Those that President Nixon saw in the parks and the Forbidden City were more animated, and on several occasions young children did what appeared to be impromptu exhibitions of their favorite games. But all Chinese who came anywhere near the President had been screened for their political reliability.

This comment from a Japanese: "Life in China is just like it was in Japan during the war—regimented, austere and quiet—no joy."

Anyone Else but Mao?

Mainland China is still poor, and in many ways backward when sized up against the more industrialized Western nations. But it has built nuclear bombs and missiles, supersonic military aircraft, and tanks. It is also thrusting ahead to build more and produce more.

This question keeps arising: Could another government, not so totalitarian in nature, have done as well? The answer, based on a relatively limited examination of China—confined to three cities, Peking, Hangchow and Shanghai, and over a time span of only eight days—is "Yes, but!"

It seems to me, having lived there for nearly ten years and having been there when the Communists finally took power, that peace inside China, more than Communist zeal or the genius of Mao Tse-tung, has been responsible for the dramatic changes.

Another party or another government, if it had been sufficiently ruthless, could have done as well. But the fact of history is that the Communists did it.

In 1949, when they took over, China was in ruins. The Japanese occupation and the civil war had destroyed the railroad system, devastated industry, burdened the country with unmanageable inflation and reduced already-low living standards to a grinding subpoverty level.

Since 1949, China has been at peace. Its armies occupied Tibet, fought in Korea and briefly in India, but no American or Indian bombs were ever dropped on Chinese cities. No armies rolled across the Chinese countryside.

The Communists introduced a reasonably effective and extremely disciplined, mostly incorruptible, government. Soviet technical aid and infusions of capital goods helped lift the economy to its feet and got China moving.

Mao introduced a collectivized society that I saw in operation—performing group tasks in the fields and workshops of the countryside, and in the large plants of the industrialized cities.

They eliminated taxes, but made prices of some consumer goods high to hold down consumption.

Control Over Minds

The Communists also introduced thought control. The effect may not be total; the Chinese are not automatons. But a continuing and pervasive propaganda campaign that relentlessly strikes at everyone, day after day, has turned a normally turbulent people into an obedient, well-disciplined mass quite unlike Chinese of the past.

You see the effects of all this everywhere. In cities I visited the Chinese were far more courteous to each other than in pre-Communist days.

I saw no shoving or pushing to gain a position of advantage in a store, or in a line waiting for a bus or entry to a "cultural palace."

One no longer hears the storms of abuse that once erupted over trivial incidents. The Chinese seem much more relaxed. The explanation may be as simple as this: Everyone has a job, even though labor in factories seems to be underutilized. Prices are set by the state so there is no bargaining. Everyone is assured of at least a basic livelihood, so there is little point in winning an advantage.

Where Are the Dead Buried?

China's landscape has been dramatically altered. The tiny parcels of land, divided and redivided over generations, have

been knitted together into communes, creating minifarms
not unlike southern California's truck farms. There are irrigation canals where none existed before.

Nowhere did I see a graveyard; I was told that all have
been plowed under to meet the vast need for tillable land.
But where are the dead buried now? I could get no satisfactory answer to this. Some, I was told, are cremated, and
others are buried on steep hillsides unfit for agriculture. But
on the vast plains of North and Central China, there are few
such steep hillsides large enough to accommodate the millions that must die each year of old age.

There is a cleanliness in the cities and in the agricultural
communes that might not impress one who had never lived
in China before. But it is striking to one who can remember
the small carts that were pulled through Shanghai's streets
every morning to collect the bodies of men, women and children who had frozen to death during the night. Back alleys
and side streets that had once been ankle-deep in filth are
all clean.

The streets are swept daily, even the alleys or *hutungs*—
side streets—far from the main thoroughfares. Block wardens
assign the task to individual households, and managers of
each store are responsible for keeping their frontage clean.

The change of living habits in the North China commune
I visited—certainly a showcase for foreign visitors—compared
with the households of the past, is almost unbelievable.
Drainage ditches drain. Individually owned pigs are penned
up and sheltered from the freezing cold. Result is that the
tiny courtyard facing each one-story, three-room mud or
brick home—the traditional dwelling of North China's peasants—is clean and free of vermin and of the roaming farm
animals characteristic of pre-Communist life.

The Western Market in the heart of Peking had, when I
last saw it in 1948, been a raucous bedlam of bargaining between buyers and shopkeepers. The floors were slippery with
mud and blood from slaughtered animals, and the flies out-
numbered people by a ratio of at least a thousand to one.

Now the Western Market is clean, but it has also lost its charm. It is only dully efficient, much as is any supermarket in the United States.

I saw no beggars in the streets and no visible signs of the prostitution that once flourished in every city.

No one with whom I talked—and they included poor pedicab pullers and the slightly more affluent taxi drivers—seems to worry about where the next meal will come from, or how their families will fare.

Birth-control devices are readily available to all families, at least in the cities, and the Chinese with whom I talked had no more than one or two children. One acquaintance said that in the rural areas it was not uncommon for a family to have five or six children. But the Chinese seem to accept the fact that small families are economically desirable, possibly because sons are no longer needed either to support them in their old age, or to worship spirits of the dead.

Old Shanghai—No More

Shanghai in the old days had been a city of wonderful sounds—a blend of quarreling and shouted insults, a loud exchange of gossip across courtyards, the singsong chant of workers pulling fearsome loads from docks to warehouses, from factories to distribution points.

That Shanghai is gone. Today the city is subdued, and only occasionally do you hear voices rising higher and higher in an excited exchange of news. Most of the docks are automated—far more so than in Hong Kong, a thriving British-ruled but largely Chinese city on the southern fringe of this country. Forklifts, small-wheel dollies and trucks have replaced coolie labor in Shanghai and the chanting no longer fascinates the onlooker. The loudest noise one hears is a loud-speaker blaring the party's gospel of the day to workers.

One heard, over the loudspeaker, the story of "Iron Man" Wang Chin-hai, who "feared neither hardship nor death, and valiantly defended and implemented Chairman Mao's revolutionary line in the three great revolutionary move-

ments of class struggle, struggle for production and scientific
experiment." Wang died in 1970, at the age of forty-seven,
but the "spirit of 'Iron Man'" is being used to inspire the
Chinese people to work harder and make heavy sacrifices.

Vanished Foreigners

In pre-Communist days, Shanghai was both home and a
well-guarded enclave for tens of thousands of foreigners—
businessmen, diplomats, representatives of various foreign
agencies. This time I saw no foreigners other than the Americans with President Nixon, no advertisements in English,
no night clubs, no gambling dens, no Western movies which
once were so popular.

Law and Order and a Drab Life

Life in today's China, as I saw it, seems to be earnest—
and rather grim. Not once did I see a funeral or wedding
cortege, nor a Buddhist or Taoist priest. Children played
together as do children everywhere. Families and groups of
young people stroll through the parks or visit the museums
and libraries—those that have reopened their doors, shut
tight during the violent days of the Cultural Revolution.

Restaurants, the cheap and the expensive, the small and
the large, all seem to be doing a good business in those cities
I visited. In a tiny Shanghai snack shop I ate a lunch of
three kinds of dumplings and a soup that cost the equivalent
of 25 American cents. The ground floor was jammed with
customers, and there were half a dozen others at the bare
wooden tables on the second floor where I ate.

Consumption of rice wine and beer seems to be on the
rise, but I saw no drunkenness in the streets or in the restaurants—a vivid contrast to the alcoholism I have observed
in Soviet Russia. Why is this? It seems to me that in Russia,
alcohol is used as an escape mechanism while in China, milder
doses of alcohol soothe and induce meditation as in the days
of Li Po, the poet. Li Po's writings, of course, are banned in
China, but wine drinking is not.

Even so, this is a highly moral and law-and-order society as far as I could see. Young men and women play poker, with no stakes, but not mah-jongg—which was gambling for high and low stakes—as in the old days.

Unlocked Rooms

The Western visitor finds himself unable to discard a bit of old clothing or worn-out equipment. Hotel employees insist that everything you bring in must be taken away. Rooms in these hotels are not locked.

I noticed, however, that Chinese often padlocked their bicycles. And a Westerner who has lived in China for years told me that many hotels have signs instructing guests to take away their valuables when they leave the room.

The "cultural palaces" and cinemas are jammed whenever performances or movies are scheduled. But the fare is rather drab, stressing revolutionary themes and glorifying the long struggle to break China free from imperialism and feudalism. The Communists do not seem to have produced anything startlingly new or vivid in drama, the dance, poetry, music or architecture.

Commented a Westerner who has been in and out of China over the years: "This is a country for budding engineers, but not for intellectuals and artists."

Women as a Fact of Life

Women's Lib is more than just a movement in China— it is a fact of everyday life. And yet it is not entirely new. Women have always been part of the labor force, and I can remember seeing them during World War II pulling light plows in the fields while the husband or father held the share straight on the furrow. Women also helped build airfields and repair dikes.

But now you find women in every stratum of society. At the top, there are women in the Communist party's senior councils. Several, including the wives of Mao Tse-tung and Chou En-lai, are members of the Central Committee. The wives of most ambassadors are party members, have held high positions in Peking and are now members of the embassy staffs.

In the factories you find women are "leading representatives"—the euphemism for both foremen and managers. Most workers in one small factory I visited were housewives, but the senior staff was male. I was told that half of the medical and dental students in China are women, but in the professional fields men seem to hold the key jobs.

It is not true that women—wearing their shapeless Mao uniforms—cannot be distinguished from men. Braids creep out of caps, and a colorful blouse can be seen peeping out of a jacket. The Chinese woman no longer walks meekly behind her husband, and she has not thrown aside all the traces of femininity. The manager of a Shanghai store said the colorful—and expensive—blouses on exhibit were not for export but were bought by women to be worn at home or under their austere outer garments.

You find Chinese men and women more comfortable together in their conversation than before. Marriages are no longer arranged and brides are not sold to other families. But I was told that go-betweens still serve as matchmakers. And the mother of a newly born girl said she could not name the baby until she had "consulted" the family. . . .

China is a land of paradoxes—and real contradictions.

There are in Peking, for instance, a number of former high-ranking Nationalist officials who "came over" to the Communists and now hold positions of prestige—but no power. Communist leaders say Nationalist officials still on Taiwan also would be welcome if they "return." But then you look at the long list of "unpersons" who formerly were high in the Communist party. I asked the whereabouts of Wang Ping-nan, former ambassador to Poland, and Chen Chia-kang, a one-time envoy to Cairo. The answer? A shrug or the laconic comment, "I don't know," or "I haven't heard."

The Chinese people revere their history and culture. Yet at Peita, the country's most prestigious university, the Chinese courses in history at the undergraduate level have been cut from seven to three. Those that survived: prehistory to the Opium Wars, the first major imperialistic assault on China; the Opium Wars to the May Fourth Movement, in 1919, the high-water mark in pre-Communist efforts to modernize and rejuvenate China; and the history of the Chinese Communist party. So the Chinese student of the history of his own country finds his efforts to examine thousands of years of recorded history restricted to three courses.

The Men With the Guns

Look at the military machine. Mao Tse- tung has written in glowing terms of war as one of the highest aspirations of man. I was told by many Chinese that their sons had but one ambition—to serve in the People's Liberation Army, and in today's China it is not a bad life even though you still hear the old adage: "Just as good iron is not forged into nails, good men do not become soldiers."

The fact is that the soldier, despite his baggy and ill-fitting uniform, is well treated in China. And as the power of the military in the nation's political and economic structure grows, so grow the chances for a private to progress in his career.

Even so, the military stays out of sight. You rarely see troops on parade and the largest unit I ever saw on the streets had fifteen men. You know the army plays a decisive role in every factory, hospital, school and commune. The Chinese themselves freely admit that. But the man with the gun is unobtrusive. And if you talk of military power, the Chinese civilian will say arms, even nuclear weapons, are for self-defense. And on occasion you will be told there are no Chinese troops outside of China's borders, and the military construction one sees occasionally inside the country is for defense—underground shelters against nuclear attacks.

Who Wears the Expensive Tunics?

The Chinese Communists say their society is egalitarian.

But who wears better-quality Mao tunics? Higher officials. Who passes out orders? Those that do are easy to spot. You don't meet the chairman of a board or a managing director; you meet the "leading member" in the hierarchy. Any close observer of Chinese society is able quickly to spot the man who is deferred to, and the one who is ignored.

Wages are far from uniform. The average factory worker is paid roughly $25 a month but, in the smaller factories, top wages may be only $18. The average worker on the commune earns about $60 a year, but the most diligent—and this includes political attitudes—can earn up to $360.

In the stores you find a similar range of values. A cheap but warm sweater costs $3.50, while a better quality one will sell for $18. A cotton-padded coat sells for $5 and a knee-length one $18.

China under the Nationalists was far from a free and open society. Left-wing writers were harassed or suppressed; the "San Min Chu I"—or Sun Yat-sen's "Three People's Principles" were considered sacrosanct. But the Nationalists permitted an opposition press and parties. There was freedom to criticize—within limits. That is not true of China today.

Name of Game: Discipline

In today's China there is regimentation on a scale that twenty-three years ago I could not imagine.

I asked a well-educated Chinese if anyone ever refused to "volunteer" for work outside office hours. His answer: "Not when it is in the service of the state."

When a snowstorm hits Peking, as it did when I was in the capital, hundreds of thousands of "volunteer" schoolchildren, office and factory workers are mobilized and equipped with straw brooms, shovels and wicker baskets. Aided by a few motorized sweepers, they work relentlessly to keep the blanket of flakes under control before it builds up to unmanageable proportions. This effort is not confined to the main thoroughfares but reaches into the side streets as well.

An acquaintance, during a long conversation about his experience in one of the new work-study camps where "thoughts" are remolded and "convictions" strengthened in training periods that can last from three months to five or more years, explained his feelings. He would not go so far as to say the experience had been a joyous one—after all, he had seen his family only once in six months. But he thought the training period was useful.

A Volunteer: "In Rotation."

Had he volunteered? He hesitated, then said: "Yes, we volunteer in rotation."

I asked a Chinese father why his son, who wanted to join the army, studied English in school. His reply: "Chairman Mao thinks a foreign language is important."

At a middle school, a young girl was asked why she studied Spanish. The reply: "I will be able to help the people of the world." How would knowing Spanish do that? "Chairman Mao says the people of the whole world are ready for revolution."

Is it possible to communicate with the Chinese Communists? The answer: Yes, if you accept reasonable limitations and have the time to make an effort.

Chinese are friendly and courteous, as they have always been. They will tell you what they believe, and many of them give the appearance of listening to what you have to say to them.

A two-hour conversation with a Chinese newsman disclosed just how far apart our worlds are—the heritage of history, culture and political viewpoints. To him, the Nixon Doctrine for getting out of Vietnam is just another face of "imperialism." Basically the President, he said, intended from now on to use Asians rather than Americans to fight Asians while protecting American imperialistic interests in Asia.

A suggestion that one way of ending the war in Indo-China would be for the United States, Russia and China to agree to end all aid to both warring sides brought this rejoinder:

"We couldn't do that. The Democratic Republic of Vietnam [Hanoi] is a brother-Socialist country and we are helping it fight American aggression."

When we parted, still on friendly terms, I said that for an American—even one who had lived in his country for years—it was often difficult to understand Chinese Communist logic. His response:

"We're not difficult. Ours is the logic of all the peoples of the world."

"We Must Keep Talking"

I look back on President Nixon's trip to China and the distinct impression I gained was that most people there—aside from the top officials—had little interest in the visit itself, or what it could mean to peace in Asia. I was not surprised by this. The Chinese, as a whole, even though many of them have been adventurers-at-sea and great merchantmen, are essentially insular and inward looking. In a country of 775 million people, most of them poor, the single individual has little time—or inclination—to ponder the subtleties of a presidential visit.

Yet the most vivid impression of all was the comment of a Chinese I had known for thirty-two years. He held my hand at the airport in Shanghai and said:

"We must keep talking or our two countries will never understand each other."

LIFE IN THE MIDDLE KINGDOM [2]

The common people of China are a strong, hardy race, patient, industrious and much given to traffic and all the arts of gain, cheerful and loquacious under the severest labor.—Lord Macartney, 1794.

[2] From article in *Time*. 99:32-4. F. 21, '72. Reprinted by permission from *Time*, The Weekly Newsmagazine; Copyright Time, Inc. 1972.

That shrewd comment by England's first envoy to Imperial China remains accurate to this day. China has long been compared, invidiously, to a colony of human ants. The fact is that the devotion to hard labor noted by Macartney is still the nation's most conspicuous characteristic. If the thoughts of Chairman Mao Tse-tung could ever be boiled down to two words, they might plausibly be *work harder*.

The emphasis on the work ethic points up one of the key realities of life in the land of Mao. Despite the social upheaval created by the revolution, there still is much of the old Middle Kingdom in China today. Although Mandarin is established as the official language, the nation's 50 major dialects and more than 1,000 variants persist in daily use. The Chinese have lost nothing in their devotion to the pleasure of the table; most foreign visitors return home several pounds heavier, spouting memories of exquisite meals. Women have been officially liberated, and are equal before the law with men; yet some marriages are still formally arranged. Young people as well as old visit burial places in rites of homage to their ancestors.

Westerners who remember the pre-1949 China, however, have been almost euphorically impressed by the transformation that communism has achieved. The people, visitors note, appear happy, relaxed and well fed. Markets and department stores are well stocked, although the prices of luxury items are almost prohibitive: a good camera, for example, costs $80. City streets are clean and orderly, and traffic jams are created by bicycles rather than cars. There is no litter, no beggars, no prostitution, no drug addiction, no alcoholism. Almost everyone wears drab, heavy-duty work clothes—children, however, are gaily and colorfully dressed—but there is no sense of utter poverty. Instead, workers and peasants alike beamingly tell Western visitors of their faith in Mao and his works, and convey a sense of happy participation in their society. . . .

However pleasing its surface appears, China's "future" is one that most Americans would find intolerable. Party control of thought and intellectual life is total. Virtually everyone works an average ten hours a day, six days a week, and sometimes the seventh day is taken up with obligatory lectures and self-study sessions. Until last December [1971], not a single new literary work of any kind other than a few poems or short stories eulogizing Mao had been published in China for nearly five years. Operas, films and drama are all propaganda pieces of Socialist realism. Life in China may be stable and secure—but it is also, from a Western viewpoint, almost unbearably confined and boring.

On the Land

China under Mao has made rapid strides toward industrialization—not just in its ability to make weapons of war but in the production of trucks, railroad rolling stock and farm machinery. (. . . [In 1971] China produced an estimated 21 million tons of steel, compared with the US total of 120 million tons.) Nonetheless, 8 of every 10 Chinese still live and work on the land. Vast rural communes, some with a work force of more than 50,000 peasants, dominate the landscape. One of Mao's principal goals has been the equalization of life in the cities and life on the farms. That he has not yet achieved. In general, housing and wages are considerably better in the cities, but in comparison with, say, the United States, even the urban worker comes off badly. A new bicycle, for instance, costs $70 to $85, but a Chinese factory worker probably would have to save two years for it, while thousands of Americans could buy it on a day's pay.

In his vivid *Atlantic* account of life in China, journalist Ross Terrill suggested that the foundation of its revolution rests on what he refers to as a "Blessed Trinity": the peasant, the worker and the soldier. A descriptive summary of their routine lives says much about what China is like today:

The Peasant

A worker at the Ma Chang Commune in Honan will rise at dawn, come rain or shine. Before a breakfast of corn dumpling soup and tea, he will spend two hours plowing the stony earth while his wife cleans their two-room hut, then joins him in the fields. A member of a three-hundred-man production team—one of six on the commune—he will then have to face three hours in the field before a brief lunch of millet, sorghum and tea. Then it is back to the fields until sundown. Before supper—occasionally it may include meat, chicken or some other delicacy—there may be time for the peasant to work on his private plot of land, on which he grows vegetables to vary the family diet and for extra cash.

On this particular commune, the pay of a peasant is 30 yuan a month—roughly $12. But the farmer pays only 1 yuan a month in rent, 6 cents to 8 cents for cigarettes and, as likely as not, nothing at all for books or magazines; despite the massive literacy campaigns, the majority of peasants are still functionally illiterate. The farmer's children, though, attend the commune school, where elementary math is taught in concrete, even ominous terms. A typical question: "How many guns have four militiamen, each armed with two guns?"

The basic foodstuffs—rice, noodles and breadstuffs—are obtained by the peasant as his share of the production of his commune, which is run by a revolutionary committee. Medical care is free, thanks to the "barefoot doctors"—medical technicians who are assigned to all communes. Television on the commune is, of course, unheard of. Many families have radios, though, and from time to time entertainment is provided by touring companies of actors and musicians.

There is a dulling sameness to the peasant's life. Still, most commune dwellers are grateful to have seen the end of the bad old days before the revolution. Then there was an eternal debt that could never be paid, abuse from a landlord whose word was law, wandering soldiers who stole and confiscated.

The Worker

To a factory worker in Detroit or even Moscow, the life of his counterpart in Shanghai or Peking would appear uncomfortably lackluster. But as the peasant in Honan sees it, his comrade assigned to an engine plant or machine shop is blessed with unimaginable luxury. Not only are wages higher than on the farms, but there are the attractions of city life—cinemas, stores, parks, athletic events—that provide some brightness to China's overall blue-gray drabness.

If a worker is single, he may share a flat with a factory colleague, and pay perhaps five yuan a month in rent. The apartment will be heated with a coal stove, if at all; the privy is outside. If he has a wife and child, a worker is eligible to move into one of the vast new government-built apartment complexes, complete with gardens and nearby day nurseries. Largely because the government controls migration to the cities, China does not have an acute urban housing shortage. A newly married couple, for example, can obtain a place to live in three or four weeks.

Like the peasant, the city worker rises early—usually by 6:30. More often than not, he lives within a few minutes' bicycle ride of his factory. The workday begins at 7:30, not at the assembly line but in the factory recreation hall, with a study session on Maoist thought. Working conditions are adequate: safety regulations spell out the proper procedures for operating machinery, for instance, but set down few guidelines for personal safety. Factories pay compensation, however, for job-caused injuries or death. Foremen tend to be chosen mainly for their job expertise, though political correctness remains important too, and the ablest serve on the factory's all-powerful revolutionary committee. Even large Western-style factories with assembly lines are not air-conditioned or heated; workers sweat in hot weather, shiver in the cold. The actual work hours are from 8:30 till noon and from 1 to 4:30; the pace, by American standards, is fairly relaxed. Unless an afternoon study session is scheduled, the worker is then free to go home.

Shopping is not a major problem. Many big stores stay open for business until late in the evening; some are open all night. As a rule, a worker's first luxury purchase after the necessary bicycle is a radio (218 yuan, or $92), perhaps a wristwatch ($34).

The Soldier

A few million homes across China are privileged to display two red banners. One says: THE PEOPLE MUST LEARN FROM THE PLA, AND THE PLA MUST LEARN FROM THE PEOPLE. The other reads: WHEN A MAN JOINS THE PLA, HIS WHOLE FAMILY IS HONORED. The posters are awarded to parents whose sons pass the stiff medical and political examinations —90 percent of applicants fail—for entry into the all-volunteer, three-million-man People's Liberation Army.

In China's distant past, a soldier belonged to the bottom level of society; these days, military service is considered an honor and a privilege. Although ready for war, the PLA, practically speaking, is a peacetime army. It has not been involved in any large-scale fighting since the brief Sino-Indian conflict of 1962, but some units engaged in sharp combat against Russian forces on the northern frontier in 1969 and there were several pitched battles with the Red Guards in the late sixties. In the wake of the Cultural Revolution, soldiers have been employed by [Premier] Chou as civil administrators, and they run everything from post offices to railroads, factories and communes.

After a recruit has passed the exam, he spends six months in basic training (mostly drill, field exercises without live ammunition, and political indoctrination) before being assigned to a regular army unit. Except for the heavy emphasis on politics, the daily routine of a Chinese soldier is much like that of a private in any army. Reveille is shortly after 5 A.M., followed by exercises, a political discussion, breakfast at 7:30, then two or three more hours of discussion before lunch. Drill is usually in the afternoon. After supper (5:30) there are two hours of farm work, followed by yet another political study session. Lights are out at 9:30. Officers and men wear almost identical gray-green uniforms.

Compared with peasants or even workers, soldiers are well fed. While on leave they are permitted to buy unlimited amounts of rationed food and cloth. Base salary is only six yuan a month, but there are allowances for families and a special food ration of fifty pounds of rice a month during the spring and autumn harvests. The normal enlistment period is three years, and can be extended for one-year terms. After his service is over, a soldier is assigned to a "rehabilitation regiment" to prepare for civilian life. Once discharged, the veteran has little trouble finding a job, either as a security officer or, if he has received technical training, in some related field. The ex-soldier automatically becomes a member of the local militia and must return to service if called. His reward for his tour of duty: a month's extra pay for every year of service, a discharge certificate and two uniforms.

The Ongoing Revolution

The ongoing Communist revolution in China is conceivably the most ambitious—one might even say the most arrogant—in human history. Its goal is not merely to transform the institutions of society but, in the words of St. Paul, to "put on the new man"—to reshape the soul and spirit of an entire people. By material standards, the achievements of this revolution are already considerable: China, for nearly a century the sick man of Asia, is now a feared and respected world power.

Like all revolutions, Mao's single-minded struggle to transform China has been achieved at a terrible cost. No one knows for sure how many people died in the aftermath of the Communist conquest in 1949, or even in the considerably smaller-scale clashes of the Cultural Revolution. Beyond that, the revolution has cruelly stultified a proud intellectual heritage that was forged almost one thousand years before Confucius and Lao Tze. All art, music, theatre and poetry that is not of and by the people—that is, a large number of the masterpieces in China's cultural history—has been destroyed or declared "corrupt" and "decadent." Intellectuals, along with landlords and survivors of the bourgeoisie, have been the chief victims of China's purges. The worst excesses of the Cultural Revolution are now over; the universities, closed for four years, have now been reopened. But who is left to teach, and what to learn? Under Mao, China has taken the daring gamble that a great nation can survive without a free-ranging life of the mind.

There are great risks inherent in so bold an effort to create a perfect, homogeneous society. One is that the dream will fail, or succeed only to the point that it reinforces the social phenomenon so well described by Karl Marx, alienation. There are signs of such alienation in the Soviet Union, in the form of youth gangs who find surcease not in doctrine but in alcohol and crime. And for all the glowing reports from shielded Western travelers, there is at least some alienation and crime in China as well: factory cities of the north are plagued by . . . youngsters who have run away from the communes and eke out an illegal existence on the streets.

The Soviet Union, although still a totalitarian society, has mellowed considerably since Stalin's death. China, too, may relax and loosen after its present leaders are gone, but the process of doing so may prove traumatic. There is risk to a would-be seamless society when its people are exposed to other ways of life, other modes of liberty. The Chinese are the most self-confident of peoples. A greater experience of Western ways may convince them that, apart from advancements in technology, there is nothing to learn or emulate. On the other hand, the human contacts that will presumably follow Richard Nixon's historic Peking venture may also raise more doubts that the road of Mao is not necessarily the road to paradise.

MAKING DO [3]

Woodshop workers at the Shenyang locomotive and rolling stock repair factory are proud of a new "technical inno-

[3] From article by Robert Keatley, staff reporter. *Wall Street Journal.* 178: 1+. Jl. 2, '71. Reprinted with permission of The Wall Street Journal.

vation" they say results from application of Chairman Mao
Tse-tung's thought, the official reason for all good things in
China these days.

Their innovation is simple: Rather than burn splintered
boards as firewood, they laboriously glue the pieces together
to make flooring for freight cars. They show off piles of
eight-foot boards, each composed of about 50 wood scraps
stuck together with resin they make themselves.

"It's not that we are short of wood," insists Chiang Ting-
hua, one of the woodshop's "responsible persons"—the vague
term often used to describe Chinese officials. "It's that workers now are masters of their country and want to make full
use of all waste materials to develop the economy."

A Shortage of Almost Everything

But, in fact, China is short of wood—plus steel, power,
capital, technicians and all other basic needs of a modern
industrial state. All, that is, except raw manpower. That's
why the key word in Chinese factories is now *self-reliance*,
the official guideline for economic growth in a nation that
simply can't afford more-wasteful Western ways. Thus, "relying on our own efforts" is the most quoted instruction of
Chairman Mao in places like the Shenyang plant.

And so far it's working. American analysts say China's
industrial growth-rate last year was 15 percent. This follows
setbacks and stagnation during the Cultural Revolution, the
mass political movement that disrupted much normal life in
China a few years ago. Premier Chou En-lai claimed recently
that among other things the nation now produces more than
15 million US tons of chemical fertilizers and 22 million tons
of petroleum yearly. These industries barely existed a decade
ago. His figures seem high, but it's generally agreed that
factory output set overall records in 1970 and will break
them this year.

"More important, resources exist for developing new industrial areas in the future," says one foreigner in Peking,
who says China recently discovered forty-four vast new coal

deposits it hasn't publicly announced. So far, in fact, most of this vast nation hasn't been properly explored by mining and oil experts. Thus, someday China may evolve into the major industrial power it wants to be, analysts say.

A Do-It-Yourself Industrialization

But that era is decades away. Meantime China is following a homemade do-it-yourself approach to industrialization; this method might have useful lessons for such poor lands as India and Egypt. Visits to factories in three widely separated areas of China give an understanding of how Chinese leaders hope that hard work and native ingenuity can overcome many material deficiencies; these are commonsense ideas that Chairman Mao pushes but that he packages in a unique brand of Marxism often confusing to foreigners.

The visits also give an idea of the enduring material difficulties as well as political problems that persist a bit more tenaciously than Peking wants to believe.

"Self-reliance" means many things in the Chinese context. One aspect is getting maximum use from limited raw materials. Another is manufacturing most, often all, necessary production equipment right in the factory rather than turning to regular makers of scarce capital goods. So-called technical innovations are also included. These often refer to adding homemade devices to existing equipment so a little extra output can be achieved. Above all, it means whipping up a kind of revival-meeting spirit combined with stricter control of the work force.

And it excludes depending on foreign suppliers for essential goods. China once depended on the Russians and had its supplies cut off for political reasons. It doesn't want to repeat that experience with any nation.

A Visit to the Shenyang Factory

The Shenyang factory illustrates many of these points. According to the Communist party theoretical magazine

Red Flag, its workers have "persistently carried out in depth a mass movement to increase production and practice economy, advancing the rapid and all-round developments there as models for other Chinese factories to copy." But a visitor also learns some things the magazine didn't mention.

The Japanese made Shenyang an industrial city during their wartime occupation of Manchuria; the city was formerly called Mukden. But the locomotive-repair plant is even older. Founded in 1926, it has grown to accommodate 9,300 workers in a dozen shops. Its main task is overhauling all sorts of railroad equipment, including steam locomotives, which China still manufactures.

Practicing economy means more than gluing together wood scraps. The factory's woodshop also saves sawdust and shavings, which are pressed into firewood. Other workers pull rusty nails from aged lumber to straighten and reuse. Some make plywood sheets from other scraps for sale to the state. They all say these activities are possible because the Cultural Revolution abolished old bureaucratic restrictions. They interrupt each other excitedly as they explain all this to a visitor.

It all adds up to an approach not economically possible in the West. By modern standards Chinese plants are overstaffed and are involved in peripheral tasks. But in China it works. The nation, with its labor surpluses and resource deficiencies, can afford to have low-paid workers rescuing bent nails and broken boards from the scrap heap. They don't have much else to do, substitute materials aren't available, and Western pricing methods just don't apply.

"It all makes no economic sense by our standards," a West European says. "But they have to do it if they want production increases. In many factories, capacity has been expanded beyond the level of raw materials available."

A Nationwide Pattern

The pattern applies throughout China. At Shenyang's No. 1 machine tool factory, metal shavings are carefully saved for resmelting. At another plant, workers retrieve waste from a metallurgical furnace. By adding water to it, they produce gas for welding. Some factories now have devices added to smokestacks for filtering out ash, but it is less for pollution control than to get material for making cinder blocks for construction.

At No. 4 northwest cotton-textile mill in Sian, workers rebuilt what they call a "grain-eating tiger"—a machine that used grain to give texture to cotton cloth. After many errors they found a way to reclaim cotton particles blowing around the factory and use them for adding body to the cloth. They claim the thick homemade goo they now use saves the state more than one million tons of grain yearly.

Another officially encouraged practice is to have factories make most of their own production equipment rather than rely on China's small capital-goods industry. One result is a collection of homemade machines, which sometimes seem inspired by Rube Goldberg.

Self-Criticism—With the Right Twist

At the Shenyang machine tool plant, one worker proudly poses by two small presses he has modified. He added a maze of control arms and other devices so the presses stamp metal automatically rather than having to be returned by hand. It looks a bit ridiculous, but it works.

And at the same city's . . . electrical-equipment plant, . . . Chang Te-ch'un engages in a little self-criticism for visitors' benefit. As chairman of the plant's governing committee, he bought a costly Swiss machine that winds copper wire for electrical components. But the machine works slowly, snaps the wire frequently and makes too much noise. Buying it was a big mistake, he says. This error caused his disgusted work staff to turn to the little red books of Chairman Mao's thoughts and vow to remedy the situation, he says.

Obviously copying key parts of the imported model, they have made simpler machines, which are supposed to work better and more cheaply. Regular production must have suffered during this process, but it seems to be an acceptable price for expanding capacity in a nation short of most manufactured items.

Mr. Chang, of course, gives it all the right political twist. "This was a great education for the plant leadership," says this official, who claims he held erroneous ideas until the Chairman's Cultural Revolution enlightened him. "We learned that the working people have boundless ability," he says.

Devising new machines doesn't mean that old ones are discarded. This is a luxury that China can't afford. Elsewhere in Mr. Chang's factory Japanese machines designed in the 1930s are still used to make plastic covers for electrical switches. At each machine, a worker must measure chemicals, insert them into a mold, operate the press by hand and then remove the new plastic case. Ten per hour is the production rate, but China figures ten of anything is better than none.

Cutting Corners

In the rush to increase output, China is cutting some corners—perhaps dangerously so at times. For one thing, safety precautions are almost nonexistent in most plants. Lathe operators seldom have eye goggles as protection against flying metal scraps. In an Anshan steel-rolling mill, huge sparks fly around the plant as visitors are shown through; a redhot particle lands in one guide's hair, but he brushes it off casually. At a brand-new fertilizer factory near Yenan in Northwest China, insulation is already peeling off pipes that carry noxious gases. The heavy smell of ammonia permeates nearby dormitories for workers in what must be a health hazard.

But the system keeps going, partly because of political policies that skillfully combine the carrot and the stick. Workers now have more say about what goes on in their factories than before the upheavals of recent years. Mass meetings are frequent, and workers are asked to make suggestions or criticisms or pass judgment on production plans.

The tactic encourages useful ideas and a broader sense of employee participation, both helpful to efficient management.

In addition, the senior staff must spend some time at manual labor. At the locomotive plant, the office staff was reduced from 1,650 to only 540 after the Cultural Revolution, and one third of the remaining staff are in the workshops at all times. It is rather like having the president of General Motors tightening door handles four months a year so he will know what it is like on the assembly line.

How to Deal With Unions

Bonuses were abolished during the Cultural Revolution, but many workers got pay raises as a result. For instance, on the Shanghai waterfront, when the bonus fund was abolished and divided equally among the workers, it meant another $2.58 a month for each. Meantime, supplies of food and consumer goods have increased, and workers can measure this change by cheaper bicycles, more vegetables and convenient medical services, now usually free. These and similar examples convince many that things are getting better, and they don't want to upset the process.

Not that they could do much if they tried, for the stick is held in reserve. Army men hold key positions at most big factories, mainly to keep political activity along true Maoist lines—such as combating any outbursts of "spontaneous tendency toward capitalism." They rely more on persuasion than on coercion, but state force is available if needed. For example, when labor unions tried to lobby for higher benefits, they were abolished. Many plants have army propaganda teams, which help organize the daily hour or so devoted to mandatory group study of Chairman Mao's works.

At Shenyang's locomotive plant, workers must study Mao for ninety minutes daily, for this plant clearly had extra troubles during recent years. "There were material incentives to poison the ideology of workers," says Hseih Ma-hsia, vice chairman of the plant's revolutionary committee (sen-

ior management group) and the only one of three former
plant directors who survived the political turmoil.

Rather reluctlantly he tells a questioner that workers
were divided into three quarreling factions. A key issue was
whether to abolish one hundred cash bonuses previously
available. Finally more than twenty members of the People's
Liberation Army arrived and restored order. They organized
a mass meeting and convinced workers that the new policies
reflected the Chairman's wishes—something few Chinese will
disobey.

Some army men are still around, although their numbers
have decreased, as is true throughout Chinese industry. In
fact, one PLA man serves as both Communist party secretary
and Revolutionary Committee chairman, the two top posts
at any plant. His predecessors were apparently demoted as
"revisionists." Mr. Chang of the plant's governing committee
is asked if some workers are happy now to be making less
money. His hurt reply: "They don't need more money because prices are stable."

Although Peking talks about "new high tides" in production, this shouldn't be confused with the disastrous
Great Leap Forward of past years, the pell-mell rush to industrialization that proved so wasteful. Production decisions
are usually made at the local level after much mass discussion, a process that seems to weed out bureaucratic stupidi-
ties. And although the forty-eight-hour workweek is standard and holidays are few, overstaffing means considerable
standing around in Chinese factories. The work pace usually
isn't frenzied.

General Easing of Tensions

And as rising production figures indicate, tensions in
most plants have eased greatly. Despite tales of mass purges
during the Cultural Revolution, most managers have survived in senior positions, possibly with titles changed. China
doesn't have enough senior administrators and technicians
to permit any large-scale firings. The new revolutionary

committees have nominally at least given about half the management-committee jobs to ordinary workers, but army men and veteran managers are still believed to exercise most power, although they can no longer ignore what Peking calls "the broad masses."

How long progress will continue and tranquillity reign is anyone's guess. "How can you motivate everyone to work hard forever without more economic incentives?" asks one US analyst of mainland economic affairs.

But a foreign diplomat based in Peking says the system seems to work better than most outsiders realize. "Many people really are newly inspired to work for the Revolution," he says. "At least enough seem to believe in it to make it last for a long time indeed."

"BECKONING A NEW GENERATION" [4]

The flood of foreign visitors pouring in and out of China today is a sardonic reminder that . . . two years ago the commentators were telling the world that China is isolated. Anything less like isolation than the Peking scene of recent months could hardly be imagined. An Australian friendship delegation had just departed as a twenty-two-man trade group from the Philippine Chamber of Commerce came up from Kwangchow (Canton), where 1,500 Japanese had attended the [1971] Spring Commodities Fair. The Philippines were followed by a similar mission from Malaysia. Princess Fatemah Pahlavi of Iran and Leila Hoveyda, wife of the prime minister, were touring in south China; in addition, a delegation from the Palestine Liberation Front was to be seen moving about in Peking. [In 1972, the influx of tourists and official visitors continued to grow.—Ed.]

Corridors of the Peking Hotel, which one week were ringing with the gay laughter of diminutive but obviously tough "model" soldiers from Laos, were the next echoing to the boisterous loquacity of seventy-six silk-suited Italian

[4] From article by Roland Berger, international trade expert. *Nation*. 213. 361-6. O. 18, '71. Reprinted by permission.

businessmen, led by their minister of foreign trade. Academicians from France, technicians from Albania, two American professors up from Hanoi, various specialist delegations from Vietnam followed one after the other. A little later, a large government-*cum*-party delegation arrived from Rumania; then came a powerful Canadian economic mission, with the minister of foreign trade at its head, and this was followed by a delegation from Australia, led by the head of the opposition party. And later still—Kissinger. [This refers to Mr. Kissinger's visit which prepared the agenda for President Nixon's 1972 trip to Peking.—Ed.]

Had Peking become the Mecca of the 1970s? What brought them all here? It seemed that, in one way or another and from their many differing points of view, all these groups and individuals felt that in this country of 750 million people and with one of the oldest of civilizations, something essentially new, indeed unprecedented, was arising. Old notions had been under scrutiny, new ideas were being put into practice, fresh concepts of social relationships were being tried, radical changes taking place in education, factory management, in the relations between town and country—all adding up to a totally new quality of life for the Chinese, who less than twenty-five years ago had been living in degradation and squalor—impoverished, illiterate, ridden with superstition and torn asunder by warlordism and civil strife. In the words, recently, of an English commentator, China is "beckoning a new generation."

Most of the visitors returned to Peking from their travels in different parts of the country with descriptions of booming industry and flourishing agriculture which I was able to confirm from my own recent visits to factories and communes in four provinces: Kwangtung, Hopei, Hunan and Honan, some of them repeats of visits made on different occasions since 1953.

The figures of national output announced by Chou Enlai . . . [in 1970] had already revealed a fast pace of economic growth. More recently, the Chinese premier remarked to

American visitors that these production statistics . . . if anything understated the position. Certainly the reports of agricultural and industrial production which have come through from thirteen of the twenty-six provinces in . . . [1971] suggest a definite leap in the Chinese economy during 1970. Hupeh, for example, in Central China, recorded a 50 percent increase in industrial production and a grain harvest up 20 percent from 1969. This province of 32 million includes Wuhan with its large iron and steel complex, heavy machine tool factories, a shipyard on the Yangtze and chemical, cement and textile plants. An increase on this scale from an already developed industrial base is no small achievement. Another province, Honan (population 50 million), claims to have raised industrial output 84 percent from 1965 to 1970. Grain production was said to have risen 10 percent from 1969 to 1970. If that is so, it bespeaks a very healthy situation in the basic food sector, for Honan is one of China's biggest wheat producers.

A new attitude of the workers to production rather than a massive program to build new *big* factories is one cause of these dramatic increases. It may seem paradoxical in the West, but the acceleration of productivity follows a nationwide attack on material inducements and the elimination during the Cultural Revolution of piece rates and bonus systems. The motivation in Chinese industry today is largely social ("Serve the People") and political ("Produce for the revolution and for international commitments"). This orientation has engendered a dynamic in the factories which not only is resulting in higher per-man output but has also induced a wave of technical innovations to get more out of existing machines by adaptations and improvements that are discussed by three-in-one combinations of workers, technicians and officials and then put into effect on the spot and without bureaucratic interference.

But perhaps the most important single factor accounting for this explosive rate of growth is the countrywide effort to develop medium and small industries, usually from scratch and based on local resources, material and human. To take Hupeh again as an example, the province in 1970 opened two thousand small local factories to manufacture, among other things, agricultural implements, tractors, diesel engines and small hydroelectric equipment. Twenty-two local chemical fertilizer factories were commissioned, and during the year construction started on a further thirty-three. In 1956 the province had only three such plants.

To study these developments at first hand I spent five days of my recent visit in the Tunghua county of Hopei province, 250 kilometers from Peking. This county of 485,000 population (it is one of two thousand in the whole of China) has responded to the call for "self-reliance" in the building of local industry in what was previously a totally agricultural area. Since the spring of 1969, thirty-one medium and small factories have started up; they use raw materials available locally and call upon underemployed and seasonally available labor, as well as bringing more housewives into industrial production. The progressive mechanization of commune farming should insure a steady supply of labor as the number of these factories increases.

In Tunghua an iron and steel plant is producing three thousand tons of iron and 1700 tons of steel annually from locally mined ore. The county operates its own coal mine; a liquid ammonia plant for fertilizer production; a miscellaneous engineering factory (207 workers) that makes compressors, electric motors and bearings; a cement works; a repair shop for farm machinery which previously had to be sent to the district center of Tangshan; a small metal factory (eighty-four workers) for wire drawing and straightening and the production of nails; a ceramic plant producing pipes for irrigation and insulators. Light industrial enterprises include a cotton mill, a paper factory (six hundred tons a year), a tire reconditioning shop, factories producing knitwear, medicines for animal and human use, mostly from locally collected herbs, and fruit bottling.

The peasants, who can call for geological advice when they need it, have combed the county—one third mountainous—and located 550 points at which minerals of various kinds can be extracted, including small but workable deposits of chrome and gold. Most of these materials will be processed by the local industry.

These local factories are practical examples of the self-reliance that has always been a tenet of Mao Tse-tung's political and economic policy, its importance being underscored by the withdrawal of the Soviet technicians and the cancellation of contracted deliveries in July 1960. The value of these local industries in limiting burdens on the infrastructure, particularly in reducing transport costs and absorbing any underemployed labor, will be obvious. The Chinese see them, moreover, as serving a social as well as economic purpose, in that they help to lower the barriers between industry and agriculture, while developing local skills and stimulating workers unaccustomed to industrial processes to find simple technological solutions. Perhaps most important, in explaining the rapid growth rates, is the speed of commissioning and the quick return on investment made possible by the relative simplicity of construction and of the equipment utilized. Frequently, as I saw in Tunghua, machines disposed of as obsolete by the big factories are reconditioned and adapted by the local workers.

An indication of the significance of these local efforts for the total economy can be gauged by statistics of cement and fertilizer production: in 1970 local industries accounted for 40 and 43 percent of national output.

Before this latest leap China had come through the shortages of the "difficult years" (1959-61) without inflation, and had by 1965 settled all outstanding internal and external debts. It had chalked up nine successive good harvests. The result has been a steady improvement in the food situation, with a national grain reserve, according to Chou En-lai, of forty million tons and with most commune brigades and teams as well as many individual households having significant reserves.

To illustrate with a grass-roots example from my recent visit. Sha-Shih-Yu in Tunghua county, whose accomplishments at industrialization I have described, is a barren, rocky hillside, its rainfall concentrated in a few weeks of the year. Until the late 1940s it was too insignificant even to have a name. In June, I saw how the lower slopes there had been transformed by the sheer task of tearing out the rocks and fashioning them into walls for terracing, then filling in with earth brought up in baskets on shoulder poles from the valley five kilometers away. It became a point of honor that no brigade member would return to the village without some earth—even the children brought a pocketful. Apple, date and walnut trees, interplanted with wheat and millet, are now growing on this reclaimed land. The result is that the commune brigade has a reserve of 37 tons of grain, with another 15 tons held as reserves by the 130 individual families. At the same time, the higher and more intractable land has been planted with pines and cypresses to stem erosion and eventually to be used as timber.

"In no small measure," said [former Secretary of State] Dean Acheson in August 1949, "the predicament in which the national [Chiang Kai-shek] government finds itself today is due to its failure to provide China with enough to eat." He added that "a large part of the Chinese Communists' propaganda consists of promises that they will solve the land problem." . . . The progress is not only quantitative; the quality and variety of foodstuffs has also enormously improved. As a result of the creation from 1958 onward, also by local effort, of fruit and vegetable communes around all cities of any size, the diets of the townspeople have changed out of all recognition.

A wide range of good quality, low-priced consumer goods is on sale in the department stores of all cities, but also in well-stocked village shops managed by the commune brigades. During my last trip I saw in many cities what, to me, was a new development—department stores that offered only consumer goods manufactured within the province, in addition to the stores that sell nationally distributed goods.

Prices of food and consumer durables are stable, tending, if anything, downward. In season, fruits and vegetables supplied direct from communes on the cities' outskirts are sold at giveaway prices. About eighteen months ago, the prices of the more commonly used drugs were slashed, in some cases by as much as 30 percent; in recent months internal air fares have come down 25 percent.

The health organizations, while still recording important breakthroughs in the more sophisticated techniques of surgery, are now focusing attention on improved services for the countryside. Whereas prior to the Cultural Revolution attempts to integrate traditional Chinese medicine (acupuncture, herbalism, etc.) with Western methods were more formal than actual in medical training, today a practical and living integration is arising out of the growth of cooperative medical services organized by the communes at the grass roots. These health cooperatives embrace the work of peasant "barefoot doctors" who, after elementary training, can deal with simple ailments, take responsibility for education in family planning and social hygiene and lead the campaign against diseases such as schistosomiasis, where local sanitation and the eradication of pests are critical. These peasant doctors provide a valuable source of recruits for the new type of medical schools that emphasize "serving the people," and particularly the 80 percent of the people who live in the rural areas. Foreign diplomats based in Peking who toured China this spring returned impressed by a chest surgery operation using acupuncture as anesthetic, the patient conscious and chatting with the surgeon throughout.

TOIL ON THE FARMS [5]

Sha-Shih-Yu production brigade is one of the 15 brigades that make up the Yueh-Gu-Guan commune, a bone-shattering 190-mile bus ride north of Peking. The brigade has 130 households, with 250 members working to produce grains, cotton, tobacco and fruit.

When I arrived at Sha-Shih-Yu, I was met by members of the commune's administrative body, the revolutionary committee. Yen Bao-hu, thirty-three, the only son in the family that had invited me to live for several days, is a member of the committee. He accompanied me to the Yens' simple three-room brick and tile house, where I met his father, a youthful-looking fifty-six-year-old brigade laborer. While all eight Yens stood shyly by—three generations, from two-year-old baby to the grandfather—I was invited to sit down for the ubiquitous cup of tea.

There were no chairs, so after some polite exchange about our different backgrounds and ways of life, we sat on the kang, a concrete box, twelve feet long and three feet high, extending along one side of the room. In the winter the kang is heated by smoke passing through it from the kitchen ovens in the next room. It is also on the kang that the whole family sleeps, stretched out on straw mattresses and pillows, which at the Yens are covered with colorful pink and white cotton cases.

The room we sat in was lit by an electric light. On two large wooden chests stood a thermos for tea, several teacups without saucers, a small white bust of Mao Tse-tung, and an alarm clock carefully enclosed in a cutout cardboard frame. On the walls hung photographs and colorful calendars with scenes from the popular revolutionary ballet "The Red Detachment of Women." A window looked out on the front courtyard where garden tools and a bicycle were kept.

[5] From article by Gael Alderson-Smith, tutor in modern Chinese studies, University of Sussex, Brighton, England. *Washington Post.* p C 1+. D. 19, '71. Reprinted by permission.

Yen Hsu-ying, twenty-two, was standing by the door near the kang. *"Wo-men huan-ying ni,"* she said, the words of welcome which a visitor to China most often hears. Then she paused shyly, obviously unaccustomed to guests living in her house. She cleared her voice, shifted her feet, and said, "Your visit makes you a part of our hearts as well as our household."

Lying in the barren valley of the Lwan River in Hopei province, near the Manchurian border, Sha-Shih-Yu has always been a poverty-stricken region. Dry, red, sandy soil, strewn with jagged pieces of limestone, makes planting extremely difficult. Rainfall is low, and the area historically has suffered from droughts of varying intensity, followed in years past by famines in which many died.

Schistosomiasis, tuberculosis and dysentery, the diseases of poverty, left the peasants weak and undernourished, and this made them prey for other diseases. Those were the days when living was a kind of dying there.

Today conditions have improved considerably, along with economic progress made by the brigade. Leveling sloping lands into hundreds of terraces shored up the region's skimpy water supply and thin soil. In 1964, the brigade's grain output totaled 535,600 pounds, nearly six times the 91,000-pound production of 1958. . . . [In 1971] with further improvements in fertilizers and the introduction of a new water-pumping system, grain production rose to 572,000 pounds.

In the communes, taxes paid to the state are fixed; they do not rise with production. As brigades such as Sha-Shih-Yu increase their output in this manner, they retain a surplus for themselves, which can be reinvested in medical, educational and welfare plans by the peasants. This is one way in which initiative remains at the local level.

The degree of Sha-Shih-Yu's success is unusual, but the problems it tackled, both in changing peasants' attitudes and in using new agricultural techniques, are common.

When the brigade in 1958 decided, after a great deal of discussion, that terracing the rock-strewn valley was the only way to combat Sha-Shih-Yu's droughts, for example, a farmer named Li Lien Yi complained that such extensive plans would require five to ten years of difficult work in which he did not want to cooperate. In the eight preceding years of cooperatives, he had joined on three different occasions, only to withdraw twice. Long-term projects in the brigade did not seem to promise immediate improvements in his life-style, and hence were not for him.

Some other farmers agreed that planning over five years was foreign to them. They also did not relish the work involved in leveling the land into terraces. But the majority of peasants agreed to the project.

Li still refused to cooperate. Some of the more enthusiastic brigade members tried to think of a way to encourage him to join them. Finally, they decided that the best way was to give him a personal demonstration of what cooperative energy could accomplish.

Li lived in a gully with two large slopes in front of his house. These isolated him; he rarely visited other brigade members and seldom took part in brigade affairs. If Li's slopes were leveled, they would turn up into the largest single plot in Sha-Shih-Yu. The more enthusiastic members decided to level Li's slopes for him.

Some farmers argued that the project would interfere with their own seasonal planting. Others, however, had become inspired by reading Mao Tse-tung's political folktale, "The Foolish Old Man Who Moved the Mountain," and believed that sweat, determination, and endurance were the keys to success. They set about mobilizing the entire brigade to level Li's slopes in the evenings.

The project took them ninety evenings. When it was done, Li was delighted by the size of his new plot. He threw his energies behind the rest of the brigade in terracing Sha-Shih-Yu's other slopes.

The sounds of a Chinese evening seem deafening. The cicadas' nocturnal symphonies echoed through my dreams only to be interrupted by the cocks' crowing and the pigs' grunting at dawn. By 5:30 A.M., most peasant households in Sha-Shih-Yu have been up and washed for half an hour. While I rolled up the straw mattress and pillow in a neat bundle at the head of the kang, I was surprised to find that the stiffness in my back, which resulted from carrying a heavy movie camera, had been loosened by a good night's sleep on the kang. The peasants claim that the even warmth of the kang protects them from rheumatism, one of their great enemies.

The Yens went to the trouble of supplying me with a white chamber pot. The outhouse, which they use, is near the main house, made of a sturdy brick and tile material. All human excrement in China's countryside is carefully saved and used as fertilizer. Some urban intellectuals, who come from the cities to help with the brigade's labors, are disgusted by the important daily job of collecting this night soil from the various outhouses, stationed throughout the village. But peasants like the Yens, who have been farming all their lives, encourage their city friends by saying the greater the quantity, the stronger the smell, the bigger the harvest.

The Yens' kitchen was long and narrow, linking the room we had tea in the night before with another one similar to it. The kitchen has a view of both the front courtyard and the rear vegetable plot. Three large wood-burning stoves flanked the kitchen walls and held cast iron, V-shaped cauldrons for cooking. Supplies and cooking utensils were stored in a corner bamboo cupboard.

Breakfasts in China usually consist of a milky rice gruel, rather like our porridge, a variety of fruits, which in Sha-Shih-Yu include apples and peaches, and occasionally some cold pieces of meat in soy sauce. Tea is still preferred as the most refreshing drink, but in large cities such as Shanghai and Peking, *chi-ahwei* (air water) is popular. This drink, which comes in lemon, grapefruit and orange flavors, is similar to our bottled soft drinks.

Dinner at the Yens might include quick-fried pork mixed with green peppers and scrambled eggs, tomatoes with sugar on top, and as a special treat, dumplings stuffed with pork and vegetables. A clear soup with bean shoots and bits of scrambled egg would complete the meal.

The Yen household typically receives payment from the commune in workpoints and in grain. One full day's labor in the fields at Sha-Shih-Yu brings 10 workpoints, which are worth 65 Chinese cents. Most peasants work a 6-day week, 50 weeks of the year, which in Sha-Shih-Yu brings approximately 210 yuan ($86.10) per person annually. Monthly wages in China range from $16.40 for the peasant in a backward area to $123 for a professor in an urban university. While the peasant on the commune pays no rent, most urban dwellers pay 2.5 percent of income in rent. Medical contributions for both urban dweller and peasant are about 41 cents per person a year. And while primary schools are free, middle schools cost $2 per term. After these basic costs have been covered, commune members' labor remuneration and workers' wage incomes are entirely their own. No personal tax has been levied in China since 1949. Pensions for those retiring at sixty-five years work out to be 70 percent of wages.

The Yens' income is increased by the cultivation of their tiny vegetable plot, plus one twentieth of an acre which is devoted to fruit trees. Private plots like these are common in Sha-Shih-Yu, as is the raising of pigs and chickens for additional family income. One fattened pig, for example, might sell for as much as $41.

The Yens have five family members working in the fields. With each earning workpoints equivalent to about $92.25 a year, the Yens can earn as much as $451.25 annually.

Workpoints are not directly cash redeemable, but are balanced against partial payment in grains, firewood, cotton, etc., as well as in cash. From their income the Yens spend about $147.60 on grain and other foods and $139.40 on clothes, repairs, and travel.

Because most basic foodstuffs are either grown in the family plot or given out against workpoints, the brigade's store contains mostly durable items. Shoe prices start at $1.20, a cotton jacket about $2.25 and the inevitable table-tennis paddle 30 Chinese cents. Cigarettes come in a variety of brands and strengths and, along with liquor, sell at nominal prices.

After its basic expenditures, the Yen family has about $123 left for savings. While this may be banked over the years, to accumulate at 3.5 percent interest in the commune's credit cooperative, the Yens may spend some of it on such major items as a bicycle at $55, a sewing machine at $28 to $56, or a radio at $20.

IV. CHINA AND THE WORLD

EDITOR'S INTRODUCTION

Although China does not rival the United States or the Soviet Union in economic or military power, its size, revolutionary zeal, support for wars of national liberation, and dominant position on the Asian mainland make it an actor of major importance on the world scene. Indeed, despite China's relative isolation for the past two decades, it has nevertheless been involved in major foreign policy issues throughout this period.

China occupied Tibet in the early 1950s and fought a brief border war with India in the 1960s. China has been involved in a bitter debate with the Soviet Union since 1960 and there have been border clashes between the two countries' troops.

China has made a persistent effort to woo the less developed countries of Asia and Africa and has implemented a modest foreign aid program to help achieve its political goals. At times, Mao's regime has presented itself as a leader of the less developed countries of the world, particularly in terms of their relations with the industrialized nations.

A number of crucial issues have directly involved the United States. Mainland China claims that it—and not the Nationalists—is the rightful ruler of Taiwan, which has been protected by the United States. American troops have fought the Chinese in Korea. China has aided the North Vietnamese in their war against the South Vietnamese and the United States. As a result, China has replaced the Soviet Union as America's prime antagonist.

This section's first article, prepared by the Foreign Policy Association, reviews US policy toward China since 1949 and serves as an introduction to some of the major foreign policy issues between the two countries. The article also offers a full review of the Taiwan question and the admission of mainland China to the United Nations and discusses the Sino-Soviet conflict.

The next selection reproduces the joint communiqué following the meetings between President Nixon and the Chinese leaders in February 1972. This document clearly spells out the differing positions of the United States and China.

The third article, written by an expert on Chinese affairs, reviews the Communist regime's diplomatic efforts in Africa and focuses particularly on two countries, the United Republic of Tanzania and the People's Republic of the Congo (Brazzaville). The article makes some pertinent observations on the character and quality of Chinese diplomacy.

The next article presents an in-depth analysis of the Sino-Soviet conflict. Written by the director of international political studies at the Hoover Institution of Stanford University, the article notes that there are many major fundamental differences between the two powers. In addition, the author speaks at length of the Chinese need for additional land, noting that the land most conveniently located for its purposes happens to be Soviet territory. As the Sino-Soviet conflict may erupt into a most dangerous confrontation, this article is extracted at some length.

The next article relates to Peking's military strategy with regard to weaponry development. The last article, which appeared in the *Bulletin of the Atomic Scientists,* presents a view of Chinese foreign policy in perspective. The author makes the point that the prime Chinese goal has been to safeguard the country's territorial integrity rather than to expand at the expense of its smaller neighbors.

OUR CHINA POLICY [1]

A new era in Sino-American relations opened last April [1971], not with the rustle of diplomatic notes or the creak of a conference-room door, but with the zing of a Ping-Pong ball. For the first time since the founding of the People's Republic of China in October 1949, the bamboo curtains parted to admit a group of American visitors.

Peking's invitation to the American table tennis team came as a stunning surprise. For more than twenty years our two countries had scarcely been on speaking terms, with the exception of periodic ambassadorial-level talks in Geneva and Warsaw. We had no formal diplomatic relations. Indeed, we refused to recognize the Communist regime as the legitimate government of the 750 million Chinese on the mainland. Ever since our military forces clashed on the Korean battlefield, China had been our No. 1 enemy in East Asia, and its military containment and diplomatic isolation were the cornerstones of our Asian policy.

In recent years the United States made some attempts to build bridges to the mainland. We tore down some of the barriers we had erected around China, and we used third-party emissaries to advise Peking that we were prepared to put our relations on a more normal footing. But our signals and messages went unanswered until the unexpected invitation . . . to the Ping-Pong players. The US reaction was immediate. On the same day that a smiling Chou En-lai, China's seventy-four-year-old premier, shook the hands of the fifteen members of the US team and three American journalists and told each one that their visit "opened a new page in relations between the Chinese and American people," Washington released a five-point program liberalizing currency, shipping, trade and travel controls. In June [1971] the President lifted the trade embargo on most nonstrategic goods. But the most

[1] From *Great Decisions 1972*. Foreign Policy Association. 345 E. 46th St. New York 10017. p 49-59. Reprinted by permission from *Great Decisions 1972*. Copyright 1972 by the Foreign Policy Association, Inc.

dramatic step toward a normalization of relations was yet to come: the President's announcement on July 15 that he would go to Peking [in early 1972].

The news sent shock waves around the globe. In a message that took no longer than three and a half minutes to deliver, the President shattered slightly more than two decades of hallowed American policy and introduced a new era in great-power relationships. . . .

At home, the announcement sparked an explosion of optimism about the future which not even the President's warnings against expecting too much could contain. But in time the euphoria subsided as critics took a closer look at the full meaning and implications of the "new China policy." Was a change in a policy which had had the support of four Presidents justified? Who would gain—or lose—the most from the proposed visit, the United States? China? or the President, by establishing himself as the "peace" candidate in the 1972 elections? Was a normalization of relations possible or desirable with a country whose sworn enemies were the "US imperialists and their running dogs"? What was the likelihood that any of the outstanding differences between our two countries could be solved unless we were prepared to make all the concessions? Finally, what effect would our new China policy have on our relations with allies and antagonists? on the outcome of the war in Indochina? On US-Soviet relations? on our relations with Japan? on the balance of power in Asia and the Pacific?

There was only one point on which the President's admirers and critics did agree, and that was that US foreign relations would never be quite the same again.

Prelude to a Thaw

For reasons which will long be debated, Peking and Washington independently but concurrently concluded last year that a thaw in relations would serve their respective interests. There had been other occasions in the last twenty-two years when either the United States or China had been willing to resume a dialogue, but until 1971 the desire had always been one-sided.

The new generation of voters is too young to remember, but there was a brief interval shortly after the Communist victory in China when Washington moved cautiously toward accommodation with the new regime. Although we did not recognize the new government immediately and opposed its seating in the United Nations, we did make a number of conciliatory gestures. We left our consular and diplomatic representatives in the cities captured by the Communists. Instead of accompanying the defeated Nationalists, led by Generalissimo Chiang Kai-shek, to the island refuge of Taiwan (Formosa), our ambassador remained in Nanking, the former capital of the Republic of China.

In January 1950 President Harry S. Truman issued a statement, frequently quoted by Peking in subsequent years, to the effect that Taiwan was Chinese territory, that we would not aid the Nationalist forces and would not become involved in the civil conflict between Communists and Nationalists. After the "dust settled," we implied, we would recognize the Peking regime.

America's conciliatory mood was not shared by the Communists. They arrested the American consul general in Mukden and arbitrarily seized American consular property in Peking, which led the United States to withdraw all its officials from Communist-held areas. By mid-1950, following Communist North Korea's attack on South Korea, US policy toward the mainland underwent a radical change. In the cold war atmosphere of the day, when the free world was feeling threatened by a monolithic, expansionist Communist empire, US leaders viewed the attack as signaling increased Communist aggressiveness on a global scale. North Korea, Red China and the Soviet Union, we assumed, acted in concert under Stalin's leadership.

In June 1950 President Truman ordered the Seventh Fleet to protect Taiwan and, in a complete reversal of policy, announced that the "future status of Formosa must await the restoration of security in the Pacific, a peace settlement with Japan or consideration by the UN." The United States resumed military aid and reassociated itself politically with the Chiang Kai-shek regime. By these actions the United States appeared to both Peking and Taipei to be intervening once more in the Chinese civil war only six months after disengaging itself.

The United States made the break with the mainland complete after the Chinese entered the Korean war in October 1950. It embargoed all trade and encouraged its allies to do the same.

Bandung Spirit

By the mid-fifties, it was Peking that was making friendly overtures. At the 1955 Bandung (Indonesia) conference of nonaligned nations, China called for "peaceful coexistence" and US-China talks. Chou En-lai subsequently offered to exchange newsmen with the United States, to open trade, even to hold a meeting at the foreign-minister level.

The United States did not buy the new soft line; quite the contrary. Our primary concern at the time was to isolate and contain the mainland through a network of anti-Communist alliances. So intense was Washington's hostility toward the mainland regime that Secretary of State John Foster Dulles, at the Geneva conference on Indochina, refused to shake the extended hand of Premier Chou En-lai. . . .

Anti-Communist passions ran high in the United States in the fifties. They were fanned by the late Senator Joseph R. McCarthy (Republican, Wisconsin) and the "China lobby" which accused the Democrats of "losing" China. Being "soft on communism" was a label which no politician who cared about his future could risk. Indeed, well into the sixties, relations with Communist China remained a politically sensitive issue. Though the government's policy gradually changed, the change was more one of tone than of substance. In 1966 President Lyndon B. Johnson termed "reconciliation" with China a desirable long-term goal. Containment was still our policy, but we were willing to settle for less isolation of the mainland regime.

The conciliatory noises that were made in China's direction produced no echoes. The Bandung spirit had evaporated, and the Chinese attitude toward the United States by the early sixties had once more stiffened. The Chinese insisted that a solution of the Taiwan issue would have to be reached before other agreements could even be discussed. By 1966 the mainland was in the throes of the Cultural Revolution, and China's isolation from the world was as much self-imposed as it was imposed from the outside. [See articles in Section II, above.—Ed.]

New Wind

The door which the Johnson Administration had opened a crack was given several strong pushes by the new Nixon Administration. Before his election, the President had indicated that he favored a change in our policy toward the mainland. In an article which appeared in the influential quarterly *Foreign Affairs* in 1967, the former Vice President and future President wrote:

> Any American policy toward Asia must come urgently to grips with the reality of China. This does not mean, as many would simplistically have it, rushing to grant recognition to Peking, to admit it to the UN and to ply it with offers of trade—all of which would serve to confirm its rulers in their present course. It does mean recognizing the present and potential danger from Communist China, and taking measures designed to meet that danger. . . . The world cannot be safe until China changes. Thus our aim, to the extent that we can influence events, should be to induce change. The way to do this is to persuade China that it *must* change: that it cannot satisfy its imperial ambitions. . . .

In his first State of the Union message [in January 1969], President Nixon called for an "era of negotiation" in place of an "era of confrontation," and it soon was clear that he had China as well as the Soviet Union in mind. In his first year in office, the President eased some trade and travel re-

strictions with the explanation that these measures were designed to further a "more normal and constructive relationship" with Communist China.

On the military front, he removed the regular US naval
patrol forces from the Taiwan Strait, called for a lowering
of the US profile in Asia—the Nixon Doctrine—and began
winding down the war in Vietnam [by announcing a time-
table for the phased withdrawal of most US combat troops—
Ed.].

The following year, 1970, the President sent the Chinese
several more peace feelers. In a toast to the visiting Ru-
manian head of state, he referred for the first time to the
"People's Republic of China," and in a December news conference he stated . . . : "Looking long toward the future
we must have some communications and eventually relations
with Communist China."

The stage for "Ping-Pong diplomacy," it appears in ret-
rospect, had been carefully set. In announcing his trip, the
President said that all nations "will gain from a reduction of
tensions and a better relationship between the United States
and the People's Republic of China. It is in this spirit that
I will undertake what I deeply hope will become a journey
for peace." That hope was widely shared, but so were some
of the doubts about the new American policy as the deadline
for the trip approached.

Was a Change Justified?

For twenty years US policy toward China was predicated
on the conviction that the Communist regime was a serious
threat to US interests and to world peace, that its leadership
was committed to attaining global influence by the cultivation and extension of power in all its forms—military, political, psychological and economic. World revolution was
the name of the game, and it was incumbent on the United
States, the only Pacific power strong enough to accomplish
the task, to checkmate China's next move.

The first evidence of Chinese expansionism, or so it was interpreted at the time, was the Korean War. Today many scholars doubt that China was actively involved in North Korea's decision to invade the south. They are convinced that China's entry into the war, following the advance of US troops into North Korea toward the Yalu, was prompted by the belief that an attack on its own territory was imminent.

The war in Indochina was seen as further evidence of that China's entry into the war, following the advance of munism was halted in Vietnam, it was argued, the cancer would spread throughout Southeast Asia and soon all Asia would be lost.

Our conviction that China was a major threat to the free world was reinforced by what were considered additional instances of Chinese militancy—of its use of force to alter the status quo: the military occupation of Tibet, the shelling of the offshore islands of Quemoy and Matsu in 1954 and 1958; the border wars with India in 1959 and 1962, and the Chinese ultimatum to India during the Pakistani-Indian conflict in 1965. Elsewhere China substituted highly provocative militant rhetoric for direct military involvement, but the goal, we were certain, was the same: expansionism and world revolution.

Hold That Line

Has there been any change in recent years in China's ideological commitments or political ambitions to justify the change in US policy? Many Administration critics believe the answer is an unequivocal No, and they are strongly opposed to a normalization of relations. . . .

The United States, in this view, must retain its military presence and sphere of influence in Eastern Asia and the Western Pacific to contain a dangerous enemy, who at this very moment continues to supply the ammunition and weapons which have been responsible for the deaths of so many Americans in South Vietnam.

Threat Reassessed

China poses no direct military threat to our interests is the verdict of other observers. US policy for the past twenty years, they charge, was built on a faulty premise, namely that China's aim was territorial expansion. . . .

The United States heightened China's insecurity, in this view, by building a string of military bases and alliances along its periphery. When our own policy was adventuristic and militaristic—when we invaded North Korea or continuously bombed North Vietnam—according to these observers, China, too, became militant to compensate for its weakness and for the blow to its pride in being unable to defend traditionally satellite neighbors. But when the United States tempered its hostility and recognized that China had legitimate interests in Southeast Asia, the Chinese reacted favorably. China, they note, played a constructive role in Geneva in 1954, and in 1962 it helped iron out the accord over Laos. . . .

The change in US policy, these observers conclude, is not only fully justified, but long overdue. They support the Administration's contention that the international order is more secure if China, as a major power, is included, rather than hostile and excluded.

Who is right? If the Administration's change of course is justified, what are the prospects that it will lead to a reconciliation of differences? One key to the answer is Taiwan.

The Taiwan Question

The chief bone of contention between China and the United States is the future of Taiwan. The United States has a moral and military commitment to the Nationalist government of the Republic of China to defend Taiwan and the Pescadores [small offshore islands]. Peking insists that we must accept its claim to Taiwan or there won't be any improvement in relations. It rests its claim on two World War II agreements—the Cairo and Potsdam declarations—

which called for the restoration of Taiwan and the Pescadores, which Japan had occupied since 1895, to the Republic of China. Despite the wartime agreements, Taiwan's status has never been clearly written into any international treaties.

Ironically, the Taiwan question is about the only one on which the Communists and the Nationalists agree. Both consider the island an integral part of China. But the question is, Whose China? The Nationalists term the mainland government illegal and a "bandit" regime and claim they represent the "real aspirations and wishes" not only of the 2 million émigrés from the mainland and 12 million Taiwanese but also "the great majority of the people on the Chinese mainland," whom they say they hope one day to liberate.

Peking, on the other hand, is determined to liberate Taiwan—the unfinished business of the civil war—and warns that it will brook no foreign intervention. It accuses the United States of having turned Taiwan into an outpost of US imperialism and insists on our removing our forces and the naval patrol from the Taiwan Strait. . . .

United States and Taiwan

US defense commitments to Taiwan are embodied in a 1954 mutual defense treaty and the 1955 "Formosa resolution," adopted by Congress at a time when the offshore islands were under intensive shelling. The treaty provides that the United States will defend Taiwan and the Pescadores if they are attacked and permits the United States to station forces on the islands.

In addition to guaranteeing Taiwan's security, the United States, between 1951 and 1965, provided Taiwan with some $1.5 billion in economic assistance. Aid was discontinued when Taiwan achieved a level of prosperity which made it a showcase among developing countries. Today Taiwan is a foreign aid donor.

Although economic aid has been discontinued, the United States still supplies Taiwan's 600,000-man armed forces with limited military aid. There are no US combat units on the island, and of the fewer than 9,000 US military personnel stationed there about two thirds are involved in repair and supply for our forces in Vietnam. Only 500 to 600 Americans are directly engaged in supporting Taiwan's defense or providing military assistance and training.

On the diplomatic as well as military and economic fronts the two countries have collaborated closely. Until last year [1971] the United States successfully defended Taiwan's right to represent China in the UN and to occupy a permanent seat on the Security Council. In return, the United States could count on Taiwan's loyal support.

The new China policy has thoroughly shaken the Nationalist government. Despite our reassurances, Taiwan is asking how much longer it can count on us to honor our commitments. For the sake of expedience, might the United States not abandon its long-time ally?

The Nationalists have many staunch supporters in this country who accuse the Administration of dumping its friends and appeasing the Communists. Other Americans, however, are of a different mind and want the United States to sever all ties to the Chiang Kai-shek regime. The acrimonious debate on future relations with Taiwan focuses on four alternative policies:

1. *One China Under Peking.* The best hope for peace in Asia is a normalization of relations with the government in Peking, which speaks for 750 million Chinese. The chief obstacle to normalization, in this view, is our alliance with the rival Nationalist government on Taiwan. The United States should abrogate the 1954 defense treaty, suspend military aid and remove its military personnel from Taiwan. There is no proof of any "credible" threat to Taiwan from the mainland. . . .

2. *Open-Ended Position on Taiwan's Future.* The determination of Taiwan's future is a problem which can only be resolved in the long run by an agreement

negotiated by Taipei and Peking. This is the Administration's present position, and it is shared by many. The United States should not commit itself to any specific political outcome, nor should it oppose a change in the present status of Taiwan, in this view. It should indicate, however, that it favors change through peaceful political process—not by force.

If the two parties refuse to sit down and negotiate, as appears likely, Taiwan might be encouraged to recognize mainland China's sovereignty, and Peking, in turn, might be urged to accept Taiwan's autonomy. . . .

3. *Full Support for the Republic of China on Taiwan.* The United States should not shirk its commitment to stand behind Taipei. We not only have a moral obligation to defend our old ally; we also have compelling military reasons to do so. When we turn Okinawa back to Japan . . . [in May 1972], a military base on Taiwan will be all the more vital to deter Communist expansionism and maintain peace in the Western Pacific. As one general expressed it, "Taiwan, in effect, is an unsinkable aircraft carrier one hundred miles from China. We'd like to keep some weapons there."

Our military presence on Taiwan poses no threat to Peking, in this view. As we have said repeatedly, our forces are strictly defensive and we would never support any move to "liberate" the mainland. On the other hand, those forces enable us to negotiate from strength. At a time when we are starting a dialogue with China, as Secretary of Defense Melvin R. Laird has said, we should not take any unilateral actions, such as withdrawing forces, which would lessen the credibility of our deterrent.

4. *Self-Determination for Taiwan.* The United States should oppose the contention of both the Nationalist and Communist Chinese regimes that Taiwan is irrevocably part of China; it should support instead self-determination for the Taiwanese.

The Taiwanese are entitled to a government of their own choosing. They are presently excluded from any role in the Nationalists' central government; it is unlikely that they would fare any differently under Peking. The United States should, therefore, support a plebiscite for the Taiwanese in which they can opt for a continuation of their present status, acceptance of Peking's sovereignty or independence.

The UN and the "Two Chinas"

The Administration's current view that Taiwan's future is "unresolved" and should be determined by Peking and Taipei is particularly distressing to the Nationalists. But the position the United States took in the General Assembly last year [1971] was opposed by both foreign capitals. For twenty years the United States had defended Nationalist claims to represent the government of China and opposed a seat for Peking. Last year it abandoned that policy and called, instead, for the "dual representation" of the two governments.

"If the UN is to succeed in its peacekeeping role," Secretary of State William P. Rogers explained, "it must deal with the realities of the world in which we live." Therefore, the United States supported the seating of the People's Republic of China in the General Assembly and on the Security Council. At the same time, it opposed "any action to expel the Republic of China or otherwise deprive it of representation in the UN."

Peking's official press agency, Hsin-hua, called the US policy a "clumsy 'two Chinas' trick" that was "absolutely illegal and futile." Taipei was more restrained but no less angry. Both Chinas insisted publicly they would not sit in the UN if the other were present.

In contrast to the furor it created in Peking and Taipei, the announcement made few ripples at home. A majority of Americans accepted the prospect of Peking's admission as realistic and, in any event, inevitable. In 1970, for the first time, the perennial Albanian resolution, calling for the seating of Peking and the expulsion of Taipei, won a majority of votes. Had the China item not been termed an "important question" requiring a two-thirds vote for passage, Peking would have been admitted then. Two close allies, Canada and Italy, had recognized the People's Republic that year, and several other countries had followed suit, thus narrowing the US margin of support.

Most Americans, according to the pollsters, agreed with the Administration that there was more hope for peace in Peking's participation in the world organization than in its continued isolation, however difficult a member it might be. Without Peking, the UN could not hope to deal effectively with a wide range of international problems affecting not only Asians but the world—disarmament, nuclear proliferation, the environment.

Keep Peking Out

A minority of citizens, however, took strong exception to the Administration's reversal of policy. Most of the reasons our representatives in the UN had cited in the past for opposing Peking's seating were equally valid in 1971, they insisted. Communist China has not promised to refrain from the use of force and therefore does not qualify for membership. To condone an aggressor is not "realistic"; rather it makes a mockery of the UN Charter and marks the beginning of the end of the UN as an effective force for world peace and stability. Far from furthering the UN's goals, Peking's presence will enable it to obstruct them. Whatever support the UN still commands in this country will be sapped.

Controversial, too, was the Administration's decision to oppose Taiwan's exclusion. Those who defended US policy termed it morally correct and politically justified. Taiwan played a constructive role in the UN in the past and was entitled to continue doing so. It had a larger population than two thirds of the UN's members. Its continued membership would not prejudice its future status.

Others were highly critical of the Administration's stand, among them the board of directors of the American Friends Service Committee.

What is at issue . . . is not the "expulsion" of a qualified member of the UN, but the transfer of China's credentials from the Taipei to the Peking government. . . . There is only one China. There should be only one seat for it. . . . The issue is proper representation in the UN for 750 million Chinese.

A majority of UN members shared this view. When the roll call was taken in the General Assembly last October [1971], 76 members voted to seat Communist China and expel the Nationalists; 35, including the United States, were opposed.

Secretary of State Rogers called the Republic of China's expulsion "a mistake of major proportion" but recognized that it represented the will of the majority. He promised that US ties with Taiwan would remain unaffected. The reaction of others was less temperate: a coalition of congressional conservatives called for immediate reprisal against the UN in the form of reduced US contributions. Though they opposed retaliation, Senate leaders of both parties appeared to agree that in the future the United States should carry less of the UN's financial burden.

The Dragon, the Bear, and the Eagle

The UN debate over the seating of the Peking regime put a number of countries on the spot, but perhaps none more so than the Soviet Union, fellow Communists, to be sure, but also China's rivals. Though the Russians voted for Peking's membership, they still could harbor misgivings about the consequences of letting the unruly fellow into the international clubhouse.

The halcyon days when the Soviet big brother took the fledgling Communist nation under its wing, supplied it with economic aid and advisers and gave it its start along the nuclear path had long since passed. The 1950 Sino-Soviet treaty of mutual friendship and alliance was collecting dust, the Soviet advisers and technicians had been recalled, and disputes over boundaries and Communist orthodoxy were the order of the day.

Today the 4,500-mile Sino-Soviet frontier bristles with armor. The largest single striking force in the world—heavy artillery, tactical nuclear weapons and 800,000 Soviet troops —is poised on China's border.

The struggle for domination between those two great empires began long before Marx and Lenin were born, but it has been exacerbated by ideological and political differences. Each country derides the other's brand of communism while seeking converts for its own. According to the Chinese, the Russians practice a "revisionist" brand of Marxism-Leninism tainted by capitalism at home and coexistence with capitalist states abroad. They are "renegades from the proletarian revolution, mad present-day social-imperialists and world stormtroopers" according to a Chinese editorial. The Russians are no less critical of communism Peking-style. In the Soviet book, it is the Chinese with their "Marxist—Leninist—Mao Tse-tung thought" who have deviated from the true faith. They accuse Mao of turning his country into a military camp.

China, anxious to play the role of a great power, feels both blocked and threatened by its powerful neighbor. Peking reportedly is concerned that the Brezhnev doctrine, Russia's rationale for invading Czechoslovakia in 1968, could one day be applied to China. Peking's leaders assert that they are prepared, but in an armed conflict China's chief defense against Soviet nuclear might would be its masses and vast territory.

The Russians, for their part, distrust China's rulers and are convinced that they are intent on wresting the leadership of the world Communist movement from Soviet hands. However, Moscow apparently wants to avoid a collision course— including another border clash which could escalate into full-scale war.

At Soviet initiative, representatives of the two countries have been meeting periodically since October 1969 to iron out border differences—so far without success. In 1970 Peking and Moscow exchanged ambassadors for the first time in four years; they also signed their first trade agreement since 1967. As Chou En-lai sees it, an improvement in state relations is possible, but the ideological conflict can go on indefinitely.

Great-Power Triangle

The Nixon policy of *détente* with China predictably created new uncertainties in Sino-Soviet relations. The Soviet reaction to the President's July 15 [1971] announcement . . . was cautious, but some concern was evident. One Moscow worry, reportedly, is the formation of an anti-Soviet alliance which could thwart the expansion of its influence in Asia and create problems in Eastern Europe. Some observers believe the Russians are also concerned that China might try to ignite a Soviet-American war.

Are Soviet fears justified? What would the United States gain from an anti-Soviet alliance? Isn't a Sino-Soviet alliance directed against the United States a greater likelihood? On the last point, most observers see little prospect of a rapprochement between Peking and Moscow in the near future, at least under their present leadership. They see even less likelihood of a Sino-American anti-Soviet alliance, given the deep-seated hostility between our two countries.

The principal advantage of a rapprochement with China in terms of US-Soviet relations, some experts believe, lies not in alliances but in its restraining effect on the Soviet Union. The mere fact that the United States and China are speaking, some argue, will prompt Moscow to act with greater caution and moderation. Others believe we should actively seek to play one power off against the other, to exploit their differences and keep both off balance. A Russia haunted by the specter of the United States ganging up with China will be more flexible and more conciliatory, these experts contend. As proof, they point to the . . . summit meeting in Moscow

. . . between President Nixon and the Soviet leaders and to three milestone agreements reached with the Russians within two months of the President's July 15 [1971] announcement: the four-power agreement on Berlin, which had been stalled for months and which, in its final form, was very satisfactory to the West; and the two US-Soviet agreements on measures to prevent accidental war, the first concrete achievements of the Strategic Arms Limitation Talks.

Other experts contend that the policy of normalizing relations with China, of dubious value in itself, can only hurt US-Soviet relations. Soviet advocates of peaceful coexistence have been discredited by what Russians consider our new anti-Soviet China policy, and hard-liners will again take the helm. Instead of accommodation, we could be entering a new era of confrontation with the Russians, in this view. Concerned about the possibility of a hostile alliance on its eastern flank, Moscow is likely to step up efforts to protect its western flank by getting the United States out of Europe. That was the true significance of the Berlin agreement, according to these experts. It paved the way for a European security conference, which will be followed, if Moscow has its way, by the exit of US troops.

For the sake of better relations with an intransigent, unpredictable enemy, these critics conclude, the United States has jeopardized a productive relationship with the Soviet Union which took years to build.

TEXT OF COMMUNIQUE [2]

President Richard Nixon of the United States of America visited the People's Republic of China at the invitation of Premier Chou En-lai of the People's Republic of China from February 21 to February 28, 1972. Accompanying the President were Mrs. Nixon, United States Secretary of State William Rogers, Assistant to the President Dr. Henry Kissinger, and other American officials.

[2] Issued at conclusion of President Nixon's meetings with the leaders of mainland China. Text from New York *Times*. p 16. F. 28, '72.

President Nixon met with Chairman Mao Tse-tung of the Communist party of China on February 21. The two leaders had a serious and frank exchange of views on Sino-US relations and world affairs.

During the visit, extensive, earnest and frank discussions were held between President Nixon and Premier Chou En-lai on the normalization of relations between the United States of America and the People's Republic of China, as well as on other matters of interest to both sides. In addition, Secretary of State William Rogers and Foreign Minister Chi Peng-fei held talks in the same spirit.

President Nixon and his party visited Peking and viewed cultural, industrial and agricultural sites, and they also toured Hangchow and Shanghai where, continuing discussions with Chinese leaders, they viewed similar places of interest.

The leaders of the People's Republic of China and the United States of America found it beneficial to have this opportunity, after so many years without contact, to present candidly to one another their views on a variety of issues. They reviewed the international situation in which important changes and great upheavals are taking place and expounded their respective positions and attitudes.

The US side stated:

Peace in Asia and peace in the world requires efforts both to reduce immediate tensions and to eliminate the basic causes of conflict. The United States will work for a just and secure peace: just, because it fulfills the aspirations of peoples and nations for freedom and progress; secure, because it removes the danger of foreign aggression. The United States supports individual freedom and social progress for all the peoples of the world, free of outside pressure or intervention.

The United States believes that the effort to reduce tensions is served by improving communications between countries that have different ideologies so as to lessen the risks of confrontation through accident, miscalculation or misunderstanding. Countries should treat each other with mutual respect and be willing to compete peacefully, letting performance be the ultimate judge. No country should claim infallibility and each country should be prepared to reexamine its own attitudes for the common good.

The United States stressed that the peoples of Indochina should be allowed to determine their destiny without outside intervention; its constant primary objective has been a negotiated solution; the eight-point proposal put forward by the Republic of Vietnam and the United States on January 27, 1972, represents the basis for the attainment of that objective; in the absence of a negotiated settlement the United States envisages the ultimate withdrawal of all US forces from the region consistent with the aim of self-determination for each country of Indochina.

The United States will maintain its close ties with and support for the Republic of Korea. The United States will support efforts of the Republic of Korea to seek a relaxation of tension and increase communications in the Korean peninsula. The United States places the highest value on its friendly relations with Japan; it will continue to develop the existing close bonds. Consistent with the United Nations Security Council Resolution of December 21, 1971, the United States favors the continuation of the cease-fire between India and Pakistan and the withdrawal of all military forces to within their own territories and to their own sides of the cease-fire line in Jammu and Kashmir; the United States supports the right of the peoples of South Asia to shape their own future in peace, free of military threat, and without having the area become the subject of big-power rivalry.

The Chinese side stated:

Wherever there is oppression, there is resistance. Countries want independence, nations want liberation and the people want revolution—this has become the irresistible trend of history. All nations, big or small, should be equal; big nations should not bully the small and strong nations should not bully the weak. China will never be a superpower and it opposes hegemony and power politics of any kind.

The Chinese side stated that it firmly supports the struggles of all oppressed people and nations for freedom and liberation and that the people of all countries have the right to choose their social systems according to their own wishes and the right to safeguard the independence, sovereignty and territorial integrity of their own countries and oppose foreign aggression, interference, control and subversion. All foreign troops should be withdrawn to their own countries.

The Chinese side expressed its firm support to the peoples of Vietnam, Laos and Cambodia in their efforts for the attainment of their goals and its firm support to the seven-point proposal of the Provisional Revolutionary Government of the Republic of South Vietnam and the elaboration of February this year [1972] on the two key problems in the proposal, and to the Joint Declaration of the Summit Conference of the Indochinese Peoples.

It firmly supports the eight-point program for the peaceful unification of Korea put forward by the government of the Democratic People's Republic of Korea on April 12, 1971, and the stand for the abolition of the "UN Commission for the Unification and Rehabilitation of Korea." It firmly opposes the revival and outward expansion of Japanese militarism and firmly supports the Japanese people's desire to build an independent, democratic, peaceful and neutral Japan. It firmly maintains that India and Pakistan should, in accordance with the United Nations resolutions on the India-Pakistan question, immediately withdraw all their forces to their respective territories and to their own sides of the cease-fire line in Jammu and Kashmir and firmly supports the Pakistan government and people in their struggle to preserve their independence and sovereignty and the people of Jammu and Kashmir in their struggle for the right of self-determination.

There are essential differences between China and the United States in their social systems and foreign policies.

However, the two sides agreed that countries, regardless of their social systems, should conduct their relations on the principles of respect for the sovereignty and territorial integrity of all states, nonaggression against other states, noninterference in the internal affairs of other states, equality and mutual benefit, and peaceful coexistence. International disputes should be settled on this basis, without resorting to the use or threat of force. The United States and the People's Republic of China are prepared to apply these principles to their mutual relations.

With these principles of international relations in mind the two sides stated that:

Progress toward the normalization of relations between China and the United States is in the interests of all countries.

Both wish to reduce the danger of international military conflict.

Neither should seek hegemony in the Asia-Pacific region and each is opposed to the efforts by any other country or group of countries to establish such hegemony; and

Neither is prepared to negotiate on behalf of any third party or to enter into agreements or understandings with the other directed at other states.

Both sides are of the view that it would be against the interests of the peoples of the world for any major country to collude with another against other countries, or for major countries to divide up the world into spheres of interest.

The sides reviewed the long-standing serious disputes between China and the United States.

The Chinese side reaffirmed its position: The Taiwan question is the crucial question obstructing the normalization of relations between China and the United States; the Government of the People's Republic of China is the sole legal government of China; Taiwan is a province of China which has long been returned to the motherland; the liberation of Taiwan is China's internal affair in which no other country has the right to interfere; and all US forces and military installations must be withdrawn from Taiwan. The Chinese government firmly opposes any activities which aim at the creation of "one China, one Taiwan," "one China, two governments," "two Chinas" and "independent Taiwan" or advocate that "the status of Taiwan remains to be determined."

The US side declared: The United States acknowledges that all Chinese on either side of the Taiwan Strait maintain there is but one China and that Taiwan is a part of China. The United States Government does not challenge that position. It reaffirms its interest in a peaceful settlement of the Taiwan question by the Chinese themselves. With this prospect in mind, it affirms the ultimate objective of the withdrawal of all US forces and military installations from Taiwan. In the meantime, it will progressively reduce its forces and military installations on Taiwan as the tension in the area diminishes.

The two sides agreed that it is desirable to broaden the understanding between the two peoples. To this end, they discussed specific areas in such fields as science, technology, culture, sports and journalism, in which people-to-people contacts and exchanges would be mutually beneficial. Each side undertakes to facilitate the further development of such contacts and exchanges.

Both sides view bilateral trade as another area from which mutual benefits can be derived, and agree that economic relations based on equality and mutual benefit are in the interest of the peoples of the two countries. They agree to facilitate the progressive development of trade between their two countries.

The two sides agree that they will stay in contact through various channels, including the sending of a senior US representative to Peking from time to time for concrete consultations to further the normalization of relations between the two countries and continue to exchange views on issues of common interest.

The two sides expressed the hope that the gains achieved during this visit would open up new prospects for the relations between the two countries. They believe that the normalization of relations between the two countries is not only in the interest of the Chinese and American peoples but also contributes to the relaxation of tension in Asia and the world.

President Nixon, Mrs. Nixon and the American party express their appreciation for the gracious hospitality shown them by the government and people of the People's Republic of China.

PEKING'S AFRICAN DIPLOMACY [3]

Among the foremost targets of the campaign of the People's Republic of China "to win friends and influence people" in Africa have been the United Republic of Tanzania and the People's Republic of the Congo (Brazzaville). Indeed, the attention level of the Chinese press to the two countries, the extent and variety of Chinese aid and technical assistance projects, and other indicators all attest that China has assigned a high priority to relations with the two states. Moreover, China's ties with both have developed without interruption since it first set up formal links with them. Not even the Cultural Revolution disrupted the process. In short, it would be no exaggeration to say that Tanzania and the Congo (B) have constituted primary focuses of Chinese policy in Africa, and that there has been a high degree of consistency in Peking's policy and behavior toward both over the years...

China's African Policy

To understand China's policy and behavior toward Tanzania and the Congo (B), one must view them in the broader context of Peking's policy toward Africa at large. This over-

[3] From article by George T. Yu, professor of political science, University of Illinois. *Problems of Communism* (U.S. Information Agency). 21:16-24. Mr./Ap. '72.

all policy has had three fundamental objectives. First, the Chinese have tried to establish and maintain their revolutionary credibility by supporting African liberation movements and new African states. Since the late 1950s, Peking has regarded Africa—with the decline of colonial empires on the continent, the emergence of many newly independent nations there, and the continuing struggle against the remnants of white rule—as one stage for the world's unfolding revolutionary struggle. Therefore, China has felt that it, as a self-styled revolutionary force, must firmly back the elements striving to bring about change in Africa.

Second, the Chinese have attempted to use Africa as a direct and indirect battleground in their fight against the United States and the USSR. This purpose has manifested itself in two ways. China has staked out a claim as the champion of the smaller countries against "aggression, control, intervention or bullying by the two superpowers," and it has supported any state or grouping which could present a challenge to the superpowers. At the same time, China has tried to incite Africans against American "imperialism" and Soviet "revisionism" and "social imperialism." Not only has it labored to "expose" the "true nature" of the United States and the Soviet Union, but it has also endeavored to identify the Soviet Union with "US imperialism," thereby discrediting Moscow's revolutionary credentials.

Finally, the Chinese have sought to bolster their own global position and prestige by securing various forms of support in Africa. Specifically, they have wanted to create an African preference for the "Chinese model" of obtaining national independence and carrying out nation-building, and to garner legal recognition and international backing for the PRC [People's Republic of China] from African governments.

Chinese behavior over the years has accorded closely with these objectives, though the situation in Africa, the constraints of China's own policy and resources, and a host of other factors have prevented the full realization of Peking's

goals. However, there have been several distinct phases of
Chinese activity with respect to the continent. The years
from ... 1955 to the onset of the 1960s constituted the initial
period. During this phase, China cautiously began efforts to
win African recognition and support—confining its undertakings for the most part to Africa north of the Sahara. By
the close of the period, it had obtained diplomatic recognition and a measure of international backing from four African states: Egypt (1956), Morocco (1958), the Sudan (1958),
and Guinea (1959).

The years 1960-65 comprised a second phase in Chinese
activity. During this time, Peking mounted a major campaign for influence in Africa, wooing nations on the continent more or less indiscriminately. At the height of this
diplomatic offensive (1964-65), Prime Minister Chou En-lai
and Foreign Minister Ch'en Yi toured the region, and China
committed a total of $190.1 million in aid to seven African
states. Two chief factors explain the level of intensity of
Chinese enterprises during the period. First, there was a
burgeoning of new sovereignties in Africa. Between January
1960 and December 1965, no fewer than 29 African colonies
gained their independence—with 16 of them emerging in
1960 alone. Second, Africa became an arena of Sino-Soviet
conflict, and the two Communist powers began competing
with growing ferocity for the support of African states on
various issues. (One of the most noteworthy instances of
Sino-Soviet rivalry involved the convocation of the abortive
Afro-Asian Conference in Algiers in June 1965.) While
China's labors during the period bore highly mixed fruit,
they did produce formal links with fifteen additional African states: Ghana (1960), Mali (1960), Somalia (1960), Tanganyika (1961), Algeria (1962), Uganda (1962), Zanzibar
(1963), Kenya (1963), Burundi (1963), Tunisia (1964),
Congo-Brazzaville (1964), Central African Republic (1964),
Zambia (1964), Dahomey (1964), and Mauritania (1965).

In 1966, Peking's activity in Africa entered a third phase,
which has lasted up to the current moment. This period has

been characterized by a reduction of China's overt presence in Africa and by a greater selectivity in China's search for friends and allies. Instead of courting the continent at large, the Chinese have concentrated on developing in-depth relations with a few states. A variety of factors probably underlay this switch in approach. Reverses that the Chinese suffered in the last half of the 1960s obviously played a part. These resulted from a combination of China's behavior, African images of Chinese policies, and the high degree of instability of African politics. Peking's militant posture and inflammatory statements during the Great Proletarian Cultural Revolution (1966-68) antagonized many African nations, and changes in government in several countries brought to power elements not at all sympathetic to China. A number of African states—e.g., the Central African Republic (1966), Ghana (1966), Tunisia (1967) —even went so far as to suspend or terminate relations with Peking. As a consequence, the total of African nations with which China maintained formal ties fell from a high of 18 in 1964-65 to a low of 13 in 1969.

However, other considerations besides reverses of this sort may have been involved in the Chinese retrenchment. By the mid-1960s, a postindependence era had dawned in Africa. Aside from Angola, Mozambique, and a few smaller colonies, the lands on the continent had all acquired their sovereignty, and the tremendous diversities that had always existed were beginning to find significant reflection in the policies and outlooks of the individual governments. Hence, some Chinese adjustment to that reality was by no means inappropriate. Since the demise of the Cultural Revolution, China has continued to stress the development of close ties with a limited number of African countries—though seven more African states have accorded the PRC official recognition since October 1970.

Both Tanzania and the Congo (B) have been among the group of African nations with which China has sought to evolve in-depth relations. Furthermore, these two African states represent perhaps the most successful of such ventures from Peking's standpoint. As the Chinese leadership sees things, China's relations with both countries have assisted it in its pursuit of two ends—securing wider official recognition and backing in the world, and combating the "aggressive designs" of the United States and the Soviet Union. For example, Peking has contended that its relations with Tanzania express the "profound friendship of the Tanzanian and African people for the Chinese people" and symbolize their mutuality of interest in ridding Africa of "imperialist" influence and in promoting African development. It claims no less regarding its relations with the Congo (B).

Approach to Tanzania

Having set Chinese behavior toward Tanzania and the Congo (B) in a general framework, let us now turn to a more specific examination of the evolution of Peking's relationships with the two. China's interest in Tanzania antedates its interest in the Congo—largely because Tanzania proved willing to enter into official relations with the Chinese first. In 1961, immediately after Tanganyika, one of the two constituent parts of today's United Republic of Tanzania, became independent of Great Britain, the new state (following the earlier example of its former colonial rulers) recognized the PRC, and the Chinese established an embassy in Dar es Salaam in January 1962. Zanzibar, the other constituent part of the United Republic, gained its sovereignty from Great Britain at the end of 1963 and also opened formal relations with the PRC. In October 1964, subsequent to the joining of the two entities the previous spring, Tanzania finally set up an embassy in Peking. Undoubtedly, the creation of official ties enabled the Chinese to bridge the communication gap that had formerly existed. It afforded them direct access to Tanzania (and East Africa), and it gave them a chance to acquire a greater appreciation of the indigenous environment and situation.

During the initial years of China's contacts with Tanganyika and Zanzibar, Chinese behavior involved more rhetoric than substance. In Tanganyika, the Chinese devoted themselves primarily to "public relations." Ho Ying, the Chinese ambassador, proved one of the most active heads of mission in Dar es Salaam within a short time after his arrival. Hardly a week passed without mention in the local press of some public act which he had undertaken. Moreover, he was responsible for forging links with other East African states. In Zanzibar, the overthrow of the Arab-dominated government by non-Arabs with revolutionary pretensions barely a month after the island won its independence encouraged the Chinese to assume a more forceful role there. China hailed the Zanzibar revolution as a victory for the people of Zanzibar and Africa, praised the new regime for demanding the removal of the US satellite-tracking station on the island, and approvingly reported Zanzibar's policy of self-reliance and land nationalization. It also carried out exchanges with various Zanzibari groups and issued joint statements condemning "the new colonialism headed by the United States." Nonetheless, Chinese support for the "revolutionary" regime took essentially the form of words, not deeds.

After the founding of the United Republic of Tanzania in 1964, Chinese activity not only changed in nature but also intensified, and Sino-Tanzanian relations warmed considerably. The number of official exchanges of visitors increased significantly. Among the Chinese who journeyed to Tanzania was Premier Chou En-lai (in 1965), and Tanzanian President Julius Nyerere traveled to China on two occasions (in 1965 and 1968). A Sino-Tanzanian Treaty of Friendship was concluded in 1965. Over the course of the years, Peking extended economic, technical, and military assistance to Dar es Salaam. . . .

Dar es Salaam's increasing commitment to the construction of its own indigenous version of "socialism" undoubtedly constituted a factor in the growing intimacy of the relationship, but of far greater apparent importance were Tanzania's internal and immediate external situations and China's appreciation of and reaction to them. Perhaps the outstanding example of this interplay with respect to Tanzania's domestic conditions involves the African state's requisites for economic development. Since Tanzania achieved independence, it has been engaged in a major developmental program; however, like other new nations, it has lacked the necessary capital and skills to implement that program. Moreover, it has encountered major difficulties in attempting to obtain external funding for developmental projects—not only because of the general retrenchment of the world's chief suppliers of aid, but also because of some of its own political decisions (such as the severance of diplomatic ties with Great Britain in 1965 during the crisis over Rhodesia's unilateral declaration of independence). The Chinese have stepped in to fill the breach—at least in part.

Through 1970, China's loans and grants to Tanzania totaled about $250 million. Loans and grants made in 1964 and 1966 account for approximately $50 million of this figure. In 1970, China provided Dar es Salaam with additional credits of $200.5 million. All the loans have been extended interest free, but while the earlier ones were to be repaid within 20 years, the 1970 one is repayable over 30 years. One can gain some perspective on the magnitude of the Chinese contribution from a few comparative data. The sum of $250 million represents about one third of China's aid commitments to Africa and roughly one sixth of all China's aid commitments. By 1971, China had displaced the United Kingdom as Tanzania's primary source of bilateral aid, and the amount of China's aid had even surpassed that of all multilateral aid to the country.

This Chinese financial aid has been allocated largely to the planning of rural development projects, the construction and furnishing of industrial plants, and the building of railroads and other elements of the infrastructure. To date, the biggest completed undertaking (in terms of money invested) has been the Friendship Textile Mill, constructed at a cost of more than $7.7 million and finished in 1968. But Chinese aid has not been devoted solely to a few show projects. It has been used to fund such diversified undertakings as the construction of fresh-water tanks in Zanzibar; the building of a bookshop, bank, and post-office complex at the University of Dar es Salaam; and efforts to control the tsetse fly in the bush of mainland Tanzania.

If one excludes the 1970 loan of $200.5 million (which was for a special project that we shall discuss in a moment), Peking's financial aid to Tanzania, while it has made possible a variety of ventures, has been far from lavish—only about $50 million. Nonetheless, figures alone do not tell the story of the value of Chinese aid from the Tanzanian standpoint. Its mere availability and the timeliness of that availability have counted for a lot in Dar es Salaam's eyes.

Two cases will illustrate the point. In 1965, Tanzania broke diplomatic relations with Great Britain (though these were subsequently renewed in 1968) over London's refusal to use force to reverse Rhodesia's unilateral declaration of independence. The British at once "froze" a $21 million loan to Tanzania, thereby putting in jeopardy the execution of developmental projects that the African nation had already embarked upon. Peking then offered to finance many of the projects with a loan of $5.6 million and a grant of $2.8 million in 1966.

The most striking example, however, has been China's commitment of $401 million to finance the construction and outfitting of the Tanzania-Zambia railway, half of that amount ($200.5 million) going to Tanzania and half to Zambia. Tanzania (and Zambia) had long sought this rail connection, but repeated appeals to the World Bank, the United Nations, the Soviet Union, and others for financial and other support for the undertaking had yielded only rejections. From Dar es Salaam's viewpoint, Rhodesia's unilateral declaration of independence heightened the urgency for the laying of the railway, for the Tanzanians felt that the reorientation of Zambia's economic links with the outside world (currently the land-locked nation's main export route was the railroad through Rhodesia) would strengthen Zambia and therefore bolster the forces of African freedom. Hence, when China in late 1965 offered to build the railway, Tanzania accepted forthwith. The formal agreement committing China to the venture was signed in Peking on September 5, 1967; the ceremonies inaugurating the actual construction of the railway took place near Dar es Salaam on October 26, 1970.

Though the economic sphere provides the most dramatic demonstration of China's responsiveness to Tanzania's internal needs, this responsiveness has evinced itself in other areas as well. For instance, Peking has rendered Tanzania technical assistance in specific realms where there has been a critical gap between local requirements and local resources. Medical personnel offers a good illustration. This category of human resources is one in which Tanzania's shortages have been exceptionally acute. As of 1969, the nation had only 502 doctors—about one for every 25,000 persons in the country. Moreover, there is a serious imbalance between medical services in the countryside and those in urban centers, for most rural areas have very limited services or none at all. In 1967, discussions about the possibility of Chinese help in dealing with the general problem got under way in Peking, and early the next year a Chinese medical team came to Tanzania to survey conditions. Chinese assistance actually began in April 1968 with the arrival in Dar es Salaam of a contingent of Chinese doctors, nurses and interpreters. It was immediately divided into smaller groups, which were then dispatched to rural portions of mainland Tanzania. While such assistance affords only partial and/or temporary solutions for the basic difficulties that confront Tanzania, this fact, from the Tanzanian perspective, does not diminish the significance of Peking's willingness to supply it.

In regard to Tanzania's immediate external situation, China's reactions have been equally sentient—in two ways. First, Peking has acted in accord with Dar es Salaam's conceptions of the way to ensure African freedom. Tanzania has stood in the forefront of African states committed to the total liberation of the continent from colonial rule. As most of Africa north of the Zambesi garnered independence, however, the stubborn resistance of the white minority regimes of South Africa and Rhodesia to majority rule stiffened, and the resolve of the Portuguese government to hang on to its colonies of Angola and Mozambique increased. Consequently, Tanzania became convinced of the necessity of guerrilla struggle for the "liberation" of these territories and has lent considerable support to the various native movements of this sort which have sprung up. Despite the fact that none of the existing movements is under the control of Communists, the Chinese have given not only moral backing but also concrete aid to many of these movements.

Second, China has helped Tanzania cope with what Dar es Salaam has perceived as a major security problem. Tanzania has a common border with Mozambique, whose national liberation movement Dar es Salaam supports. Since the Mozambique rebellion first broke out, the Portuguese authorities in the colony as well as the Rhodesians and South Africans have possessed military superiority over Tanzania and could conceivably subject the country to reprisals, subversion, etc., to try to thwart its activities in behalf of the rebels. These and other conditions persuaded the Tanzanian government that it ought to build up a military establishment, and China has aided in this effort.

Chinese military assistance to Tanzania commenced in 1964; since the termination of the Canadian-Tanzanian military assistance program in 1970, China has become the principal source of military hardware and training for the African nation. Detailed data on the Chinese contribution have never been revealed, but a few general things can be said about it. China has provided military instructors to train Tanzanian military officers and new recruits locally, and it has transported specialized personnel—e.g., marine police, other naval personnel, tank crews, etc.—to China for instruction. It has also supplied arms and matériel, including small

arms, tanks, trucks and patrol boats. In 1969, President
Nyerere reported that most of the nation's "armyware"
came from the People's Republic of China and that Tanzania
would continue to "receive Chinese military instructors."

In sum, Peking's sensitivity to Tanzanian needs and its
response to them have constituted the chief reason for the
expansion of Sino-Tanzanian relations. Thus, what successes
the Chinese have registered in the African land may be said
to reflect the astuteness of their statecraft—their careful pursuit of their goals in consonance with local circumstances.

Dealings With the Congo (Brazzaville)

Let us now pass on to an analysis of the evolution of the
PRC's relations with the Congo (B). These began most in-
auspiciously. At the dictate of the relatively conservative and
pro-French President Fulbert Youlou, a defrocked priest with
strong anti-Peking sentiments, the Congo, upon gaining its
sovereignty in 1960, rejected Peking's recognition and instead established diplomatic ties with the government of the
Republic of China on Taiwan. It continued to maintain
these ties until after Alphonse Massamba-Debat replaced
Youlou as head of the Brazzaville government in the wake
of what became known as "the three glorious days" (of revolution) in August 1963. Once the French recognized the
Peking regime in January 1964, the new Congolese government transferred its recognition from the Republic of China
to the PRC, and an exchange of missions soon took place.
A Chinese embassy was opened in Brazzaville in June 1964;
a Congolese embassy was set up in Peking the succeeding
September.

The relationship warmed quite rapidly. In July 1964,
China extended a $25.2 million loan to the Congo. The en-
suing October, the Congo's President Massamba-Debat visited China. During his stay . . . , he signed four agreements
with the Chinese on behalf of his nation: a friendship treaty,
an agreement on economic and technical cooperation, an
agreement on cultural cooperation, and an agreement on

maritime transport. During subsequent years, the frequency of high-level official exchanges between the two states mounted steadily. In 1965, for example, Chi P'eng-fei, then Chinese vice minister of foreign affairs, traveled to Brazzaville; and in 1967 Congolese Prime Minister Ambroise Noumazalay attended the October celebrations in honor of the founding of the PRC. The overthrow of Massamba-Debat in July 1968 and the installation of a new government headed by Major Marien Ngouabi merely heightened the trend. In early August 1968, less than a month after the change of regime, an official Chinese delegation led by Huang Hua, then ambassador to the United Arab Republic and the only Chinese ambassador who had not been recalled to China as the Cultural Revolution gathered steam, showed up in Brazzaville to participate in the celebrations marking the anniversary of the August (1963) Revolution. . . .

China's relations with the Congo, particularly since President Ngouabi's assumption of power, have sometimes been characterized as resting on ideological foundations. There is, to be sure, an element of truth in this observation. China and the Congo communicate with one another and the world in the language of Marxist ideology; both repeatedly echo such themes as the call to struggle against imperialism and against new and old colonialism and the necessity of an alliance of Asia, Africa, and Latin America in the unfolding world revolution. Moreover, Ngouabi has promised to use Marxist-Leninist principles—i.e., to follow "scientific socialism"—in shaping his domestic programs, and in December 1969 he declared the Congo a People's Republic. But the Congolese leader by no means fits the model of a steeled Marxist-Leninist, though the Chinese have referred to his assumption of power as representing "a step further in the Congolese revolution." Nor does his government pursue a line consonant with Chinese prescriptions for remaking society. One must, then, look deeper for the basic reason for the flourishing of the relationship.

As with Tanzania, the main factor seems to have been the Congo's internal and immediate external needs and Peking's response to these. In the domestic sphere, the Congo's requirements for economic development afford one illustration. The country has been heavily reliant upon France for financial and technical assistance; however, Brazzaville has felt that it cannot necessarily depend upon French aid forever. In addition, such great reliance on France tends to give Paris considerable leverage with respect to the Congo's internal course. Hence, the acquisition of other sources of help has been highly desirable from the Congolese viewpoint.

By and large, the amount of Chinese loans and technical assistance has been small. Through 1970, China's promised financial aid totaled $25.2 million. These credits were extended in the 1964 loan mentioned earlier, which was to be interest free and repayable within ten years. Thus far, the Chinese have actually funded only a few projects. The largest single one is the Koussoundi Textile Mill, whose construction was begun in November 1966 and finished in May 1969 at an estimated cost of $4 million. Others in process or completed include a shipyard for fishing boats, a state farm, and a survey for the construction of a hydroelectric power plant. China has rendered technical assistance in several areas. Among the more significant contributions have been the training of workers at the Koussoundi Textile Mill and the supply of medical personnel. The medical program was started in 1966 and expanded in 1967. Most of the Chinese medical teams that have been furnished under it have been dispatched to the undeveloped northern interior.

In no sense, then, has China become the dominant outside force in the Congo's economic picture. In every year since independence, for example, France has provided Brazzaville with at least $10 million in aid; furthermore, over the entire postindependence period, the European Economic Community has given the African country an additional $50 million at minimum. Of note, too, Paris has continued to back the Congolese currency, and Brazzaville has remained within the franc zone. The worth of Chinese financial and technical aid from the Congolese standpoint, however, has not lain primarily in the size of the contribution. Instead, it has derived from the demonstration to Paris that, despite French dominance in the Congo, Brazzaville is not without other friends to whom it might turn in the event French largesse ceased or French demands in return for continued help became excessive.

Perhaps the most important realm in which Peking has fulfilled the Congo's domestic requirements, however, has been the political rather than the economic. Over the years since 1963, and particularly since President Ngouabi assumed power in 1968, the Congo has suffered from political instability as a result of fierce competition among Congolese political and tribal groups for power. After Ngouabi seized authority in 1968, for instance, he sought to govern the country by means of a coalition embracing the army, the Congolese Labor party, and a few other specific political and tribal groups, but he has faced strong challenges from groups outside that coalition. As a matter of fact, between 1968 and 1970 there were no less than four abortive coups against his regime. For this reason, the elements in control of the Congolese government have tended to look to various foreign powers for support against their local enemies in order to maintain their rule. China has been one of these powers, and while Peking has undoubtedly been troubled by the political instability in the African nation, it has faithfully lent its backing to the existing government. (It ought to be stressed that Peking's policy in this case cannot be taken as implying an endorsement of military coups and military regimes as such or a readiness to forge ties with any regime which recognizes the PRC. In all probability, the Chinese leadership merely preferred in this instance the certainty of relations with a friendly regime in power, whatever forces it represented, to the uncertainty of throwing China's weight behind dissident elements. Broadly speaking, China has distinguished recognition and maintenance of relations with African states from recognition and support of African "liberation" movements, and as separate policies the two should not be confused.)

Chinese political support of the Congo government has taken various forms, both symbolic and real. For example, Peking has denounced the series of attempted coups against the . . . regime and attributed each to "subversive and sabotage activities instigated by United States imperialism and its running dogs." Moreover, it has cited them as proof that the United States is endeavoring to crush the Congolese revolution—that the "new and old colonialists" and the "imperialists" are striving to arrest the progress of the African revolution—and that the leaders of Africa must exercise vigilance to overcome the temporary difficulties. . . .

Apropos of the immediate external circumstances of the Congo, the Chinese have shown themselves keenly attuned to Brazzaville's sense of threat from its neighbors—chiefly the Republic of Zaïre, as the former Congo (Kinshasa) is now known. This sense of threat reached its zenith in 1970. By that juncture, the current ruling groups in the Congo (B) had become convinced that President Joseph Mobutu's regime in Kinshasa had had a hand in the various attempts to unseat President Ngouabi. Indeed, an attack upon Brazzaville in March 1970 had been launched from the Zaïre capital, and the rebel commandos had called upon President Mobutu to send paratroopers to aid their cause. As China has viewed all the regimes in Zaïre with a jaundiced eye since the demise of the rump Lumumbaist government of Antoine Gizenga in 1961, it has had no qualms about supplying the Brazzaville authorities with military assistance.

Our information about this military assistance is exceptionally limited, but China is known to have offered military aid to the Congo beginning in the late 1960s. In 1971, the two countries signed a military-aid agreement. This provided, among other things, that the Chinese would supply the Congolese army with heavy equipment and would train Congolese military specialists in China.

All in all, however, it must be admitted that the Chinese reaction to . . . [Brazzaville's] external situation is far less critical in accounting for the growth of Sino-Congolese ties than is the Chinese response to the African state's internal situation. The Congo's national security has never really been seriously threatened from without, for the African country has retained special relations with France and has no neighbors that enjoy overwhelming military superiority. Moreover, it has taken steps recently to ease tensions with its neighbors and has thus enhanced its security. . . . During 1970, Brazzaville also acted to improve relations with Kinshasa. Whatever the relative importance of the internal and external factors, however, this in no way diminishes Chinese appreciation of and response to Congolese conditions as an explanation for the blossoming of the Sino-Congolese relationship.

Conclusions

What conclusions, then, do these two case studies suggest? . . . First, the high value that China has attached to relations with Tanzania and the Congo (B)—as evidenced by the resources that Peking has invested in improving them—stems not from the intrinsically vital character of either country to China, but from the functional roles that the two play in China's overall foreign policy. By contributing to Tanzania's and—to a lesser extent—the Congo's domestic development, for example, China has established itself as a source of economic and technical aid for African lands and, in so doing, has given evidence of its own national capabilities and power. In rendering military and related forms of support to Tanzania, one of the principal forces behind the push for Africa's total liberation, Peking has tended to substantiate its claims of commitment to that cause. By extending strong moral backing to the government of the Congo, which the Chinese have depicted as a state repeatedly subjected to "imperialist subversion and sabotage," China not only has drawn attention to its self-proclaimed role as a champion of small-country opposition to "superpower oppression" but has also highlighted Peking's view of the general shape of international politics at present. Since no African nations loom large in Chinese strategic calculations, any intimate relationship which China has evolved or might evolve with another individual African land is likely to rest on the same kind of foundations.

Second, the fundamental reason why the Chinese have managed to fashion strong ties with both Tanzania and the Congo (B) lies in a combination of the two countries' needs and Peking's sensitivity and response to these needs. To be sure, the political elites of the two African states have displayed a certain degree of ideological affinity with the Chinese. The Tanzanian government, for example, has voiced dedication to the creation of a "Socialist" society, and it has not hesitated to borrow specific programs and ideas from foreign sources, including the Chinese, whenever it deemed these suited to its own goals. By the same token, the Congolese government, at least since President Ngouabi acquired power, has announced its intention to pursue the path of "scientific socialism" and employs a Marxist vocabulary to describe its undertakings. But in neither instance has the ideological factor been the overriding one. Sino-Tanzanian relations have flourished because China has shown an appreciation of Tanzania's developmental and security requirements and a willingness to help satisfy them; Sino-Congolese relations have likewise thrived because Peking has recognized not only the Congo's developmental and security requirements but also the Brazzaville regime's requirements vis-à-vis its internal enemies and has been ready to assist in meeting them. In light of this evidence, it seems probable that future Chinese successes in both these and other African nations will depend heavily upon local circumstances and needs and the ability of the Chinese to perceive and react positively to them.

Third, the burgeoning of China's relations with Tanzania and the Congo has resulted from Peking's grasp of the differences in the situations confronting them and its employment of specific foreign-policy instruments suitable to each context. In other words, the Chinese have demonstrated appreciable flexibility in their handling of relations with the two states.

This observation raises the larger question of the Chinese leadership's perception of Africa generally. The two cases examined suggest that, rhetoric aside, China has developed an appreciation of individual variances on the continent—that she can distinguish between conditions in one land and those in another, select an appropriate response for each instance, and choose the most efficacious tools to accomplish her purposes there. To make further gains in Tanzania and the Congo as well as other African countries, Peking will most certainly have to exhibit such capacities in even greater abundance than it has heretofore.

THE PERMANENCE OF CONFLICT [4]

There are no facts that render continuous Sino-Soviet conflict or a Sino-Soviet war a necessary or predestined event. If by enchantment cooperation-oriented regimes were to appear in Moscow and Peking, and if large sums of capital could be made available to solve economic problems in Siberia and China, the two countries could collaborate very fruitfully, ending a contest dangerous to both. But this alternative to the situation exists mainly in our imagination. In the real world, the Sino-Soviet conflict exists and has been progressively growing worse. Given the nature of the present Moscow and Peking regimes, which are imperialistic, the two party-states will prove unable to cooperate effectively. Hence problems and divisive factors will not disappear; indeed they

[4] From "Peking and Moscow: the Permanence of Conflict" by Stefan T. Possony, director of the international political studies program at the Hoover Institution, Stanford University. *Modern Age*. 16:130-45. Spring '72. Reprinted by permission.

will proliferate. The chances are small that this conflict will be liquidated peacefully.

On the other hand, a destructive war does not seem to be in the interest either of the USSR or of China. The Soviets should be more reluctant to fight a drawn-out mass war than the Chinese, but this implies that they must consider using preventive nuclear strikes. While both Communist states probably will incessantly maneuver and each will attempt to install a friendly regime in its opponent's land, they will most likely try to remain within the parameters of political and subversive warfare.

Still, the conflict has its own logic and momentum and it may force war decisions on one or the other side. . . . Specifically, the more suspicions, fears, complications, and ambitions the Sino-Soviet conflict generates, the more heavily will nuclear weapons, through their mere existence, weigh on the balance between war and peace. In 1914, many reasons brought Britain into the war against Germany, but the one overriding reason was British fear that Germany's growing naval power would destroy the British world position. It would be entirely in line with historical precedent if the USSR decided it could not forever coexist with Chinese nuclear weapons.

American strategy must, therefore, be geared not only to the factual existence of the Sino-Soviet conflict, but also to the unpredictability of its further development, as well as the probability, high or low, that it could culminate in war. The constellation does not, by any means, exclude temporary alliances: the United States must be ready to defend itself against the USSR and China combined. Alternately, the United States might enter a temporary alliance with either power. We are dealing with a triangle of hostility in which each of the three powers is opposed to the two others. But in this triangle the intensity of the various hostilities may vary by time and place.

Experience shows the fragility of constellations and the reversibility of alliances. Regardless of what we believe the intentions and policies of our opponents to be, we must primarily worry about their capabilities. Hence we draw the conclusion that we need very superior armaments to discourage any temporary alliance against us by the Chinese and the Soviets. The United States must be strong enough to handle both Communist superpowers. We also must guard against acts of provocation which either of the other "triangulists" may attempt in order to involve us in conflict with his competitor. In a triangular relationship each "triangulist" always attempts this third power role. This is an elementary fact which Americans often ignore.

If the Soviets succeed in placing their man at the helm in Peking, this may mute the conflict for the time being, but it would not liquidate it. It also depends partly on US policies whether the Sino-Soviet conflict continues without major eruption.

The US conflict with China lacks many of the usual geopolitical dimensions that weigh on conflicts between neighbors. Hence a political change in Peking might liquidate mainland China's hostility against us. Not so with the conflict between China and the USSR: the triangular conflict relationship is not fully symmetric.

The Sino-Soviet split is often interpreted as an ideological squabble limited to disagreements concerning communism. If this were so, the conflict could be liquidated promptly by adjustments of the ideology which, on both sides, is highly flexible. Yet ideology is just one of many factors. And even the same ideology would have profound differences in meaning in countries with such different socioeconomic infrastructures and cultural traditions.

Both the Maoists and the Soviets profess socialism (or communism) as their overall political religion, just as Christians, Jews, and Moslems profess monotheism. Both ruling parties proclaim Marxism-Leninism as their own species of the genus socialism. This is comparable to our general belief in Judeo-Christian values. On the next level the USSR professes Leninism in a neo-Stalinist mode, while mainland China professes Leninism in a Maoist interpretation. . . . A religious simile would be the split between Catholics and Protestants. . . .

The behavior of the Soviet and Maoist elites has amply demonstrated that their ideology is a strongly motivating force and that global implantation of a Socialist-Communist social order is a most serious intent. . . . In both cases, the expansionist tendencies continue age-old imperialist trends and commitments. Russian imperialism is derived *inter alia* from a very ancient religious source—namely, eastern Catholic orthodoxy and the Byzantine tradition. China's expansionism was always related to firm convictions about culture and Chinese superiority and it is tied to the notion that China should control all areas over which it once exercised "suzerainty." The Maoists do not argue that China should be reconstituted in its maximal historical frontiers, but in its frontiers of the eighteenth century, before territories were lost. Among the incorporated and tributary lands taken from China are Afghanistan, Kashmir, Mongolia, West Turkestan, Tannu Tuva (Tuvinsk Autonomous Soviet Socialist Republic), and the southern portion of the Soviet Far East; the Maoists also have occasionally claimed Kamchatka. Some calculations show that since 1689, China has lost about 4 million square kilometers of land. Some 50 percent of this territory was taken by Russia; 40 percent was located in Southeast Asia and the Himalayas. The rest consists of Korea and Taiwan.

Whether the objective of global ideological victory commands priority in strategic decisions is another question. Undoubtedly, an objective of this sort imparts direction to long-range and permanent policies. If it did not, it would be merely rhetorical. But the preservation of state and regime must necessarily exercise overriding priority, especially in regimes that have lasted for some time. Priority also is a function of opportunity. World conquest may be assigned top priority at a time when there is a good chance that this objective can be attained. Once a major expansionist objective exists and is adhered to consistently, it will always influence policy and under suitable conditions may become the controlling motivation. Consequently, such an objective must never be belittled, let alone disregarded.

The CCP [Chinese Communist Party] and the CPSU [Communist Party of the Soviet Union] collaborated closely for many years. Without Soviet help, however grudgingly given and however often denied, the CCP could not have conquered China. (US help also was a crucial factor.) But it is not true that the CCP invariably obeyed the Kremlin's orders and functioned as a Moscow puppet. Mentally and physically communications between the two parties often were extremely difficult. The CPSU had to rely on Westerners for liaison with the Chinese Communists and the CCP lacked trained people to familiarize the Russians with their problems.

The early leaders of the CCP were very confused ideologically and their immediate successors were more or less unthinking imitators of Moscow. In 1935 . . . Mao Tse-tung usurped control over the party and embarked upon his own "line." He did not by any means leave the orbit of the Communist International, but he struck out on an independent course. As early as 1936, he indicated he was not going to "liberate" China in order to turn over control to Moscow, and he also argued that the Soviet experience was only in part relevant to the Chinese Communists.

In 1938 Mao insisted that the Chinese Communists study Chinese history, adjust Marxism to Chinese conditions, and get rid of dogmatism. Party members who returned from study in the USSR were warned to be critical about what they had learned, and in several instances were subjected to reeducation. In 1939, in a major policy . . . [divergence], the CCP was audibly critical of Stalin's pact with Hitler.

In 1945 the CCP committed itself fully to the ideas of Mao Tse-tung. Mao was credited with having given to Marxism-Leninism its Asian form. This commitment to Mao implied the rejection of Stalin's ideological monopoly, and it also involved a downgrading of Lenin. While the ideological split began in 1945, it was not at first accompanied by an operational split. On the contrary, the Soviet contributions to Mao's conquest of China between 1945 and 1949 were indispensable. But the Soviets were skeptical about Mao and from time to time indicated that they regarded his ideas, not as Communist, but as bourgeois viewpoints. The stories that Stalin did not want Mao to seize power are no doubt true.

After coming to power the Maoists followed the Communist routine of nationalizing industrial and agrarian capital and of instituting collective property and a centrally planned economic system. Yet from the start the Asian Communist parties were aware that the differences between the CCP and the CPSU were major and were arguing about the Soviet and the Chinese "roads." East European CP's avoided publishing some of Mao's works—in East Germany (1951) a few speeches in which Mao discussed ideological issues were suppressed.

The twentieth CPSU [Communist Party of the Soviet Union] congress in 1956, when Stalin was posthumously dethroned, was a significant turning point in the relations between the two parties. Thereafter, one programmatic Maoist text after the other was issued to deepen the ideological differences. In 1958 the Maoists began publishing *Hung Chi* (Red Flag), their own ideological organ. In 1964 the Maoists talked about the "pseudocommunism" of Khrushchev and called the new rulers not only revisionists but class enemies engaged in carrying out capitalist restoration. This particular line completed the divorce between the uneasy partners.

The ideological differences bear mainly on problems of strategy and war. About nuclear war *Hung Chi* presented an expurgated version of the statement which Mao had been making repeatedly to the effect that even excessive losses did not matter if in the end communism would destroy imperialism. The Maoists did not agree with Moscow's coexistence strategy which they wanted replaced by a strategy based on "proletarian internationalism." They rejected the idea of peaceful seizures of power; and they wanted to carry out the world revolution through national liberation movements, which indeed is a substantial departure from, if not a reversal of Marxism. . . .

In 1964 the Maoists declared . . . that Communists make revolutions . . . and added that the world revolution must necessarily be violent. This line was at variance with Marxist orthodoxy, even as preached by Lenin, especially since it was coupled with enormous emphasis on the revolutionary role of the peasants. It contradicted the basic Marxian doctrine that communism presupposes advanced industrialization in the capitalist mold and that technology creates the preconditions wherein revolution becomes necessary in order to continue economic progress. . . . The notion that Maoist strategy is the correct model for all Communists is utterly unacceptable to the Kremlin and especially its nuclear planners. Why, they argue, must violence be regarded as necessary when in some instances it can be replaced by subversion and political maneuvers?

Peking contended that Moscow's strategy is too timid. By contrast the Kremlin fears that Peking's strategy may entrap the USSR in unmanageable crises and ruin the world revolution. The deeper dimension of this dispute is, of course, that the two "comrades" now are talking about two different things—Moscow means a world revolution which results in world rule by Moscow, and the Maoists plan a world revolution that extablishes world rule by Peking. This is not a new situation in history. "My cousin and I are in full agreement," Charles V said about François I. "We both want Milano."

Not surprisingly the Soviets have asserted that according to Maoist teaching, Marxism really is inapplicable in China. They insist that Maoism implies forced labor, the limitation of consumption to the satisfaction of elementary needs, and the restriction of thinking to the contemplation of Mao's ideas. The Soviets also argue that in China the individual is nothing but a cog in the state machinery, that there are no democratic institutions in mainland China, that all resources are utilized to arm the state for "great-power politics," and that there is personal instead of party dictatorship. All of this is true of Maoist China and to a large extent of the Soviet Union as well. The Maoists counter that Soviet communism degenerated after the death of Stalin, a mutation exemplified by the rebuilding of a class society under Khrushchev. According to the Yugoslav Communist Milovan Djilas, however, the class society reemerged with all its trimmings long before Stalin died. A class society it is and always was, and the Maoist Communists have called upon the people in the USSR to rise against the Communist regime which is exercising class exploitation over them.

The Maoists uphold the principle of equality among all Communist parties and states; that is, they refuse to accept any overlordship by the CPSU or the USSR. Neither the Russians nor the Russians together with the other nations that are supposedly federated within the USSR possess the capability of ruling the Chinese, whose self-government, whether they are unified or partitioned, is an irremovable fact of modern history.

The ideological differences between the CPSU and the CCP may not exhibit deep philosophical meaning, but they advert to the fundamental truth that China remains beyond Kremlin control and constitutes a major block to further Soviet expansion. The Kremlin is quite unable to remove this obstacle; it may succeed in weakening China, but only at the cost of weakening itself and the USSR. . . .

The two main Communist powers are divided by numerous additional problems. Some of those deserve listing:

1. A most important difference between Red China and the USSR is that there are successful Chinese anti-Communist states, the Republic of China on Taiwan, as well as Singapore and Hong Kong. These states have demonstrated that the Chinese have a genuine choice of systems better than Maoist communism.

2. The Republic of China has preserved the political legitimacy of Free China and has maintained a powerful national and anti-Communist Chinese army. The Kuomintang, which has been the traditional foe of communism, also has shown, what the Maoists failed to do, how the negative traditions of ancient China can be overcome and how Chinese society can be modernized. On Taiwan China possesses a substantial cadre of people who are qualified to take over, participate in, or run, the government and administration of the entire Chinese nation. The anti-Maoists and anti-Communists on the mainland, who have fought the dictatorship from within, will need the help of persons who have gained experience in modern government and management, and especially development. Free China has done infinitely better than Maoist China, and this fact is known to the people on the mainland.

In contrast, the several millions of Russian refugees have remained, by and large, politically impotent. Dispersed all over the earth and split into many groups, they never set up an organized, coordinated and meaningful opposition to the Kremlin. They even failed to develop authentic and comprehensible theoretical alternatives to communism that would reflect Russian traditions, be geared to the future problems of the country, and also respect the interests of the non-Russian peoples and citizens of the USSR.

3. The regime in the USSR is a functioning entity, even though not very efficient. The Mao regime is anarcho-Communist and disorganized, and fails to meet even the low standards of government that the USSR is providing. It is possible that China may split into several satrapies.

4. In the USSR the Red Army never wielded real political power. From time to time the military have been influencing decisions but the party always retained the controlling position. By contrast, the PLA has become the real power in mainland China and since the Cultural Revolution it has been running the CCP, or what is left of it. Whether this situation will change after the ejection of Lin Piao, only the future will tell.

5. Considering the size and population of China, the PLA is a comparatively small army. It is not unified like the Red Army but to some extent has remained "factionalized" and tied to regionalism. As central government weakens or the political formula changes, centrifugal tendencies will grow stronger. Moreover, the PLA simply may lack the strength and the motivation to keep the country together; its commanders are obvious targets for Soviet political warfare. Chinese chances of influencing Soviet military leaders are minimal or nonexistent.

6. The CCP suffered badly during the Cultural Revolution and may not recover from its predicament. It actually split into two parties, not counting the PLA. Few of the leaders enjoy party or mass support, and the party structure and power pyramids are unstable. The party has been good only at propaganda and commotion. It remains unable to give the leadership which, despite its faults, the CPSU still provides.

7. Both Communist parties are on particularly bad terms with the peasants. But in China the peasants (or the dwellers in the countryside) account for four fifths of the population, as compared to a shrinking two fifths

in the USSR. The density of the peasant population still is excessive in China, while the Soviet countryside is beginning to experience depopulation.

8. The economic failure of the Mao regime is astounding. Maoist China offers the unique example of a major contemporary economy which has been stagnating. While some growth—perhaps one fifth or one sixth of the comparative growth achieved on Taiwan—may be stipulated in the absence of reliable figures, the lack of real growth is more or less self-evident, despite a few eye-catching successes, e.g. the nuclear and aerospace industries. On a per capita comparison China operates on a level roughly one tenth of that prevailing in the USSR.

9. Both countries have multiple "national problems," but those of the USSR are more significant and potentially explosive. National problems affect about 40 percent of the territory and half of the population of the USSR, and half of the territory of China but only a small percentage of the Chinese population. The Sino-Soviet and Mongolian borders divide the Turkic and Mongolian peoples, hence both countries have some identical national problems, which tend to aggravate the mutual tension.

10. The internal situation on mainland China is unique and in no way comparable to that of any other Communist state. The internal situation in the USSR is unsatisfactory but not unstable; that of mainland China is both highly unsatisfactory and highly unstable.

11. The USSR is well into its fourth leadership generation, and two demographic generations have passed from the scene since 1917. The Communist regime in China still is run by its first generation of leaders, but that group is about to disappear. When it does, power struggles will be intensified. . . .

The USSR does not want a final and basic break with China, as a result of which its Asian frontiers would be rendered dramatically insecure. It needs a safe position in Asia and for this purpose requires Chinese collaboration or impotence. The puzzle is this: how can the USSR attain those objectives?

Despite conflict and difference, the systems of the USSR and Maoist China retain important similarities. Both systems are totalitarian but neither, as constituted now, is likely to continue forever, or even for a long time. In both countries, the Communist party has degenerated: the middle ranks are status-quo-minded bureaucrats, no longer conquerors or innovators. In both parties and countries the young people are looking for new approaches.

In both parties, there are severe and ever-recurring intraparty power struggles. Both parties—their top echelons and presumably their successors—are committed to direct and indirect expansion and permanent revolution. Both want to destroy "capitalism" and defeat the main capitalist-democratic countries. Both Communist regimes have been practitioners of mass purges and murders. In the USSR, the purge mania has declined appreciably, though concentration camps remain; in Red China terrorism still is in full swing. Both economic systems fail to satisfy popular needs and both are managed according to antiquated and unworkable concepts. In both regimes, agriculture is in perennial crisis, the peasants are the most exploited "class" of the society, and agricultural outputs remain far below requirements.

Soviet social development has now reached a stage where dictatorship—that is, rule by a few poorly informed people running a huge country by decree as well as rule by people who can be purged but not replaced in orderly fashion—is becoming a roadblock. Mainland China is less developed than the USSR and, therefore, could temporarily benefit from an authoritarian, knowledgeable, and wise government. But its large size and great complexity, as well as the extraordinary ignorance of most of its rulers, have caused the dictatorship to act as an effective brake on virtually all advances.

Unbalanced development is one of the main features of the Soviet economy. The USSR is simultaneously one of the most highly industrialized and also one of the more backward areas in the world; mainland China is simply backward and essentially a subsistence economy. But the Soviet economy and industry are very large in sheer size. China remains a poor farming country with a few factories and several very large cities. The USSR is able to support a major war for a long time. The economy of Red China, with its lack of surplus, may be able to support irregular warfare indefinitely, given a truly strong national morale, but it cannot support regular war. It can fire nuclear weapons but it cannot yet accomplish conquests against well-armed opponents.

The Soviet economy has been unable to solve major problems of planning, e.g. economic calculus, balancing of offer and demand, pricing, distribution, investment, marketing, consumers' satisfaction, etc. Further economic progress is predicated on substantial organizational reforms. By contrast, the Chinese mainland economy's primary need is for major infusions of capital, for the development of infrastructure, and for the elimination of bureaucracy from agriculture.

Border disputes may serve to mask a larger quarrel, e.g. warnings may be conveyed through shallow penetrations by small detachments. Hundreds, possibly thousands, of incidents occurred along the ill-defined Sino-Soviet border during the 1960s. The Soviets, to improve their access to China, seized a number of border crossings, such as bridgeheads, fords, and mountain passes, while the Chinese tried to recover some of those positions and also engaged in reprisals. The series culminated in 1969 with two battles fought about an island in the Ussuri [a river in the Pacific coastal area]—the island is uninhabited and has no intrinsic value.

Actually, the so-called border dispute is not related to river islands and poorly marked borders, but deals with huge territories. The Chinese do claim a few thousand square miles of islands and mountain passes, but they are really demanding the return of something like 1.5 million square miles of Soviet territory in Eastern Siberia and the Pacific coastal areas, and they also want the return of some 300,000 square miles in Central Asia. They want to deprive the USSR of 10-15 percent of its lands. The Chinese also desire the Mongolian Republic (600,000 square miles).

Normal border disputes are susceptible to compromise and arbitration. Disputes about large territories are customarily settled by war. If such territories are of strategic significance, war is the only method of settlement. The Soviets argue that China's natural frontier is defined by the Great Wall and that Chinese possessions beyond the Wall, e.g. Sinkiang, Inner Mongolia and Tibet, were gained by imperialist conquest. The USSR does not claim Chinese territories, though Soviet Turks and Mongols could stake out such claims. But the USSR questions Peking's right to rule nearly one half of its present land holdings.

From the Soviet point of view, the issue of this border dispute, which was initiated by Peking, is whether or not the USSR remains a Pacific power or indeed a multinational and Asian empire. From the Chinese point of view, the issue of this controversy, in which the USSR acts like a "great-power chauvinist" and not like a fraternal Socialist state, is whether or not China gains access to lands and raw materials which she needs and which were formerly hers. This brings up the much disputed question of whether China is or will be overpopulated and whether she must expand to keep her population adequately fed and supplied.

The Soviet Far East is inhabited by 5 to 6 million people. . . . The total area has a surface of 4.6 million square miles. . . . Of this area, the Chinese assert a claim for at least one third. During the last thirty years, the Soviets have managed to put altogether one million additional inhabitants into this region, which could be what British Columbia is for Canada. Much of this immigration was from eastern and western Siberia, which are short of manpower, and there was substantial emigration away from the Soviet Far East.

By contrast, the population of Manchuria has been increasing by 1 million a year—every year during a sixty-year period. About 100 million Han moved toward the north during this century—one of history's largest migrations. In the south of China population growth was more rapid than in the central provinces, which given the present economic-technological pattern, are overpopulated. There has been during this century a vast Chinese emigration southward and overseas. If the borders were opened, there would be an avalanche of emigrants, not just anti-Communists, but of people seeking work and economic success.

During and after World War I there took place a substantial Chinese and Korean *Unterwanderung* [infiltration] into Siberia and the Soviet Far East. In 1939 some 90,000 Chinese were living on the Soviet bank of the Ussuri river and were interbreeding with the Udege, the native people. In the same area there were 100,000 Koreans who remained endogamous; another 70,000 Koreans were living in the Chinese-claimed Ili river valley and other parts of the Kazakh SSR. The Soviets urgently need workers in the area and in all party congresses since 1956 this point has been stressed. There is no question whatever that the buildup of the Soviet Far East is lagging badly.

Is China overpopulated? The question is difficult to answer: the meaning of the term is ambiguous. Also, the population of China is unknown, and so is its growth rate. But it is known that the caloric food intake is fairly low (2,000-2,100 calories per day) and that high-quality foods are scarce. It is also known that the Maoist planners aimed to double food production and that at best they achieved a static per capita output. There is no need in a modern economy for a country to produce its own food. But to be a regular food importer, the country must be a regular exporter. To do this China would have to accelerate industrialization, drawing workers away from the fields into the factories. For the time being, therefore, China can only be a marginal and occasional importer of food, but it must buy food whenever it has a bad harvest.

Accordingly China must increase food production. This requires expansion of cropland and substantial improvements of agricultural yields. Exact figures are lacking but there is good evidence that Chinese yields are mediocre; that most croplands are particularly deficient in nitrogen; that unused arable soils are scarce, perhaps nonexistent; and that new land can be cultivated only after it has first been ameliorated.

There is plenty of land available and plenty of hands to do the necessary leveling and to build canals. But large amounts of water must be transported over long distances of mountainous terrain. Vast constructions are needed, and a manifold expansion of fertilizer production, including the development of a fishmeal industry, is mandatory. Furthermore, the modernization of agriculture requires fast progress in electrification and motorization. Thus, huge capital investments are indispensable. The effort would consume much time during which the population will continue to grow and to build up pressure. . . .

China has always been a land of regional famine—statistically it usually produced enough food but the surplus from good harvest areas could not be transported into areas suffering from drought or flood or insects. Transport deficiencies still are among China's major problems and they still prevent the effective distribution of food.

The possibility that the Chinese may be a *Volk ohne Raum* [people without room] has been feared for about one hundred years. This possibility is now turning into a reality, possibly a nightmare. A Maoist production plan for 1960 called for an output of some 450 million tons of grain by 1967. Chou En-lai claimed that production in 1971 reached a record of 264 million tons, unquestionably an "overestimate" by some 20 percent. When the population reaches one billion by 1990 or so, some 600 million tons will be required. This would require a boost of 230 to 300 percent within twenty years.

It is clear, therefore, that acreage increases by 10-20 percent, a mere doubling of fertilizer output, and even plenty of short free-flow canals—changes that are within current Chinese capabilities—will not solve the problem. A four- or fivefold increase in yield from the present cropland may be technologically or theoretically possible, but lack of capital makes it *economically* unfeasible. . . .

China must prepare to feed a population of one billion by 1990 or at the latest by 2000 A.D. Assuming per capita food intake to remain static (at a highly inadequate level of something over 2,000 calories daily), China with its present technology would need 170 million hectares, including double-cropped fields. There is not much arable land left in the densely populated portion of the country—the usual estimate is 3 percent. Assuming there are still 12.5 percent available, an additional 15 million hectares could be cultivated. To utilize more land in the western steppes and semidesert areas would require enormous investments, but if 8 percent of the total unused arid lands were cultivated—a highly optimistic idea—5 million hectares would become available. Perhaps an additional 30 million hectares of the enlarged cropland could be used as double-crop fields—equally an optimistic hope. With all these changes, China's cropland would still be 30 million hectares below requirement. If yields were boosted by 20 percent, the deficit would disappear, provided the population stabilizes.

Since those assumptions are far too hopeful, the deficit, even with a static per capita food intake, may easily reach a level of 50 million hectares. The compensating yield increase of one third to one half would require substantial enlargement of foreign trade. If food intake were to be doubled—a cautious requirement—the deficit would be above 200 million hectares. This deficit could be overcome only if yields were at least doubled. This may be feasible, but above a certain yield, FAO [Food and Agriculture Organization of the United Nations] figures show, increasing amounts of fertilizer are needed to raise output by small increments. To judge from Taiwan figures, about a twentyfold increase in tilizer are needed to raise output by small increments. To China's yields. . . .

Heavy fertilization, of course, must be accompanied by large-scale irrigation, or else the soils are damaged. In a hilly country where, as in China, even steep slopes are being cultivated, this poses additional technical and economic problems; for example, a nationwide irrigation system would augment power requirements drastically. Unless major resources are made available, a doubling of yields by 2000 A.D. seems out of the question; even an increase of 50 percent would be a major accomplishment.

Realistically, therefore, China is short of perhaps 100 million hectares (250 million acres), less if the Chinese content themselves indefinitely with lean diets. Where could China find such large tracts of land? Obviously, the cultivation of the marginal lands left on hilltops in eastern China won't help very much. So if land is to be found within China, it must come from the western part, excluding the Tibetan highlands. It may be remembered that the arid lands in western China carried relatively large populations in centuries past. The area has become the heartland of the Chinese nuclear industry, and the heavy influx of industrial manpower, settlers, and soldiers already is straining existing resources, especially water, very badly. . . .

So the question arises whether China can find land outside of its borders. Burma would be one promising place, and it would be suitable, possibly for cultivation by southern Chinese. Burma is sparsely populated, and it has about 17 million hectares which, with two and one half crops annually, would be the equivalent of 42 million hectares. Since 6.5 million hectares are cultivated, the net gain could be 26 million hectares.

The Mekong river project [a vast scheme attempting to exploit the potential of this South East Asian waterway] will result in an additional 9 million hectares for double-cropping. The significance of this project is heightened by the fact that with new "miracle rice," yields can be multiplied. Therefore, China's rice requirement can perhaps be satisfied—if the new seed is also sown in mainland China and if China obtains a large portion of the Southeast Asian rice output. Yet Southeast Asia is difficult to conquer; it has its own rapidly growing population, and it offers few suitable locations for Chinese peasants to plow the soil. Hence, that area's resources must be secured through amicable trade; and this implies that the interests of the local population will retain first priority. In any event, rice is not the only requirement China must satisfy. In fact, the qualitative improvement of the Chinese diet, which is a precondition of all-around economic progress, presupposes considerable diversification.

Mongolia has a surface of approximately 1.5 million square kilometers, of which the southern third is part of the Gobi desert. It also has high mountains where cultivation seems unfeasible. Yet something like one half or about 80 million hectares should be agriculturally usable, and much of the country appears suitable for the nuclear plowshare treatment. Even now Mongolia has the beginnings of a crop agriculture and it carries vast herds of animals. If the pastural lands could be improved—this is in part a matter of irrigation—there is no reason why Mongolia could not become the Argentine of Asia and sustain in addition to more than 20 million horses, camels, goats, and sheep, plus expanded crop cultures, at least 50 million cattle rather than the 2-million-odd it is handling now. Since Mongolia is virtually empty, it is the biggest agricultural prize in East Asia. The USSR is holding this large piece of real estate to which it has no title whatever and which historically was linked to China. Aside from the ethnic problems involved, China really needs that land, not as a subjugated country, but as a part of its economy.

The Chinese-claimed areas in the Soviet Far East include, perhaps, 30 million hectares of arable land. This may be an overestimate: but what is arable in that area depends in large part on the manpower, the capital and the technology that can be invested. At best 10 percent of the arable land is now cultivated and enormous work (e.g. drainage) would be required to put more under the plow. . . .

The USSR is expected to reach 333 million inhabitants plus-minus 25 million by 2000 A.D. The contested areas in the Far East will be populated by 20 to 30 million people at most, many of whom will be transients. Yet Manchuria alone will hold more than 120 million. While the Soviets are developing Chinese-claimed areas in western Turkestan rapidly, the buildup of the Soviet Far East, decreed by the twenty-third CPSU Congress in 1966, is slow and uncertain. The Soviets are, of course, fully aware of the fact that their Pacific territories are economically needed by China and Japan. Since they form an integral part of the Far Eastern economic region, they must be regarded as a distant colony of "Russia."

The Soviet Far East, even in its southern parts, is not a very promising cropland but there would be enough to sustain a population of more than 50 million, provided modern techniques (for example, up-to-date permafrost management) were used. The *taiga* [coniferous forests in the far northern regions of Eurasia and North America] is expensive to ameliorate, but it is next to the tropics the world's main unused agricultural reserve; and the Chinese are virtually the only people who could use the *taiga* on a large scale. For the time being, the *taiga* is agriculturally more promising than the steppe and particularly the desert.

Among the potentialities of the "second Manchuria" in the *taiga*, prospective crop yields are *not* of crucial importance, even though some staples like soybeans, millet, rye, and potatoes are well adapted to the area. With some amelioration, the southern *taiga* could carry livestock in large numbers; and with the exception of pigs, China lacks live-stock. If China gains access to Mongolia, the *taiga*'s livestock contribution might not make too much difference, but the area is uniquely rich in fisheries, and China needs far more fish. Above all, the area has enormous timber stands, and China is notoriously short of timber.

Livestock, fish, and timber offer a solid basis for indus-trial development. The USSR has gone in heavily for food processing, paper manufacture, and shipbuilding, but the area's energy potential invites really ambitious projects. With its Soviet tributaries Zeya and Bureya, the Amur is rated at 10 million kilowatts, or 1.2 percent of the potential energy in all of the world's rivers. The area also contains oil, gas, and coal. There are ferrous and nonferrous metal deposits which could sustain considerable industry....

Even as it is known today, the potential of the area ap-pears to be crucial for China, the USSR, and Japan. There are constraints on rapid development; mainly, lack of man-power, transport, and cheap food. Food would be cheaper if it were brought in over short distances or grown locally; and transport improvements presuppose extensive rail- and road-building. But the brutal fact is that the necessary manpower can be supplied by China only.

China's involvement in the "second Manchuria" rests on three factors:

1. The main population pressure in China is vectored toward Manchuria and points across the Amur.

2. The development of the "second Manchuria" would be expensive but this is one area where plenty of cheap manpower can do a maximum of good.

3. The first and second Manchurias are geo-econom-ically interrelated. The development of the area north of the Amur actually is predicated on the resources avail-able in the area south of the river. Conversely, the accel-erated development of China's Manchuria requires eco-nomic interaction with the territories held by the USSR.

China's first order of business is to solve its agricultural problem to ensure feeding its population and to get industrialization effectively on the road. Without agricultural solutions, no industrialization; but without industrialization, no agricultural solutions. Thus, China needs additional land but it cannot obtain or use that land without quantum jumps in capital investment and technological capability.

The Chinese lack a satisfactory raw materials base and therefore they covet the return of territories which contain coal, oil, natural gas, iron, tin, lead, zinc, and gold, and which formerly were owned by them. Economic pressures and territorial needs are related to ethnic cleavages in China, the USSR and in Southeast Asia.

When Japan is brought into this game, the situation becomes still more complicated. The Chinese don't have to expand but the less effectively their problems are being solved within their current boundaries, the stronger their urge to conquer will be. . . . The Chinese are the most populous nation on earth; their number is growing steadily. Yet they remain restricted to a confined habitat, much of which is today economically useless.

There will be somewhere a critical point, but whether it will come when China has 1 billion or 1.2 or 1.5 billion inhabitants, is unpredictable. Population growth and delay in resource development already may have carried the country beyond the point of no return. Hopefully there is still time. But are there sufficient resources to use the period of grace? Is the constellation suitable to problem-solving approaches? The answers to both questions must be hesitant and pessimistic.

SHIFT IN STRATEGY BY PEKING IS SEEN [5]

Senior American analysts believe China is rapidly building an arsenal of tactical nuclear weapons and special air-

[5] From article by William Beecher, staff correspondent. New York *Times*. p 1+. Jl. 25, '72. © 1972 by The New York Times Company. Reprinted by permission.

craft designed to deter a major Soviet military thrust across
the long border, or to throw up a nuclear defense if deterrence should fail. [For an analysis of the Sino-Soviet conflict
see "Chinese Foreign Policy in Perspective" in this section,
below.—Ed.]

A basic shift in Chinese defensive strategy appears to be
under way, they say, basing this assessment in part on the
following indicators:

China has tested a number of relatively small nuclear
weapons ranging from 10 kilotons to 30 kilotons each
that can be delivered by a tactical fighter-bomber of Chinese design, known in the West as the F-9.

She is now mass-producing the F-9 at a rate of about
fifteen a month, and of the 300 produced over the last
two years, at least 200 have already been placed in operational squadrons.

China seems to be abandoning her old defensive concept of deploying primarily poorly equipped militia and
paramilitary units along the border to draw Soviet divisions deep into Chinese territory before attempting to
engage them with regular troops to the front and guerrilla
units to the rear.

Instead, the analysts say, she has recently been moving
several first-line army divisions and air force squadrons
to forward positions, suggesting an intent to challenge
seriously any Soviet advance at an early stage, before it
could penetrate deep into industrial Manchuria, for
example.

These developments, viewed separately, had evoked mild
interest on the part of Government officials concerned with
China.

But, in a series of interviews, well-placed sources at the
Pentagon and other agencies said they were convinced that,
when taken together, these events showed that Peking had
decided that the unrelenting Soviet buildup of large-scale
conventional and nuclear-war forces along the border was

so menacing as to require a fundamental shift in China's military and diplomatic strategy.

The diplomatic shift resulted, among other things, in China's invitation last year [1971] to President Nixon, who until a short time before had been vilified as one of China's worst enemies, for a historic state visit.

The move toward conciliation with the United States, analysts note, may serve to make Moscow less confident of how Washington would react to a Soviet nuclear or conventional strike against China. In addition, they say, by removing even the very remote possibility of an American-supported return to the mainland by the forces of Nationalist China, it permits Peking to transfer some of the considerable forces it had long maintained in fixed defensive positions on the coast across from Taiwan.

Three Tests Held in Two Years

The recent military redeployment and weapons tests suggest to some officials that China is actively preparing to employ nuclear weapons, if forced to do so. In such a case, they say, she apparently wants to be able to hold major Soviet troop concentrations in sparsely settled border areas, so as to reduce nuclear fallout and other collateral damage to Chinese cities in the interior.

While no one in the West can know for certain, it is conservatively estimated that China has at least fifty to one hundred tactical nuclear weapons in her arsenal. Other estimates range two to three times that high, based on the fact that China now has three plants turning out uranium and plutonium of a grade suitable for producing weapons.

China's last three nuclear tests—the only tests she held last year and this—were all of relatively small weapons. One last November and another in January were reported to be under twenty kilotons, equivalent to the force of 20,000 tons of TNT. Atomic weapons of about that size destroyed Hiroshima and Nagasaki in World War II.

The most recent test, which like the two others was set off in the atmosphere, was in the range of 20 kilotons to 200 kilotons, according to the Atomic Energy Commission.

Before those tests, the previous two, one in 1969 and one in 1970, were of three-megaton weapons, equivalent to three million tons of TNT. These weapons were believed to be designed for use both by TU-16 medium bombers and on intercontinental ballistic missiles that were under development.

The focus on small tactical nuclear weapons in the last few years suggests to some officials that Peking is more eager to come up with a quick counter to what it perceives as the immediate menace represented by the Soviet border buildup, than concentrating now on warheads for its missiles.

China now is believed to have deployed a total of fifteen to thirty 600-mile medium-range missiles and five to fifteen 1,500-mile intermediate range missiles. Her first 4,000- to 6,000-mile intercontinental ballistic missile has apparently not yet been test-fired at full range.

Missile Deterrent Dubious

It will be several years at best before Peking will have enough ICBMs to threaten seriously the one hundred defensive missiles the Soviet Union is permitted to deploy around Moscow under its arms limitation agreement with the United States. Thus deterrence must be based more immediately on other forces.

China's small force of missiles and TU-16 bombers could destroy cities such as Vladivostok in Soviet Asia in retaliation for a first strike by the Russians, but analysts suggest that Peking may not be sanguine about deterring Soviet leaders with so limited a capability, particularly when most of the missiles and bombers are vulnerable to surprise attack.

CHINESE FOREIGN POLICY IN PERSPECTIVE [6]

Ever since its inception, the People's Republic of China has been regarded by many in this country and elsewhere as irrational, bellicose and expansionist, posing a "mortal danger" not only to her neighbors in Asia but also to the whole world. This perception quickly prompted Washington to isolate Peking diplomatically, strangulate it economically and contain it militarily. For some twenty years the United States pursued this policy with such seriousness and determination that it saw fit, among other things, to escalate steadily its direct military intervention in Indochina in the belief that the local insurgencies were actually covert Chinese aggressions which must be resolutely halted. But while the Indochina war was still in progress, President Nixon stunned the world on July 17, 1971, with the announcement of Henry A. Kissinger's secret journey to Peking and the President's own acceptance of an invitation from Premier Chou to visit Peking before May 1972. [The visit took place in the last week of February 1972.–Ed.] Clearly, the President's momentous new approaches to Peking indicate that the long-standing policy of all-around confrontation with the new China is giving way to one of negotiation and mutual accommodation. Equally clear is that this drastic change in policy would not have occurred had there not been a basic alteration in the President's assessment of Peking's intentions and conduct in the international arena. . . .

What have been Peking's international goals? One, and certainly the most important of them, is to safeguard the territorial integrity and political independence of the Chinese nation. The sanctity of this goal can be better appreciated if one recalls the fact that the rise of the Chinese Communist movement itself was a result of the Chinese people's quest for an effective way to cope with foreign encroachments and domestic disorder.

    [6] From article by Franklin W. Houn, professor of government at the University of Massachusetts. *Bulletin of the Atomic Scientists.* 28:15-21. F. '72. Reprinted by permission of Science and Public Affairs, the Bulletin of the Atomic Scientists. Copyright © 1972 by the Educational Foundation for Nuclear Science.

The Maoist determination to protect China's territorial integrity and political independence, it should be noted, has not prevented Peking from making compromises or even practicing self-abnegation if the stake is relatively small, in order to serve better China's long-run national interest—if it is done of her own volition. The seven hundred square miles of territories that Peking handed over to Pakistan under the border agreement of March 2, 1963, is a notable case in point.

However, Mao and his colleagues now appear to be determined to preserve China's sovereignty in all the outlying regions, including Sinkiang, Tibet, and Taiwan. For historical, legal and practical reasons Communist Chinese and non-Communist Chinese alike regard these territories as integral parts of China. Since these territories have been among the major targets of foreign encroachment in modern times (Russia had designs on Sinkiang, England brought Tibet under her influence and Japan occupied Taiwan), their retention has taken on a symbolic significance to the Chinese. Thus the reported Russian attempts to sow dissension among the national minorities in Sinkiang, the Indian and Western desire to create an "independent" Tibet, Washington's and Tokyo's plans for establishing "two Chinas" or "one China and one Taiwan" and the assertion that "the status of Taiwan has not yet been settled" have been looked upon by the Chinese not only as a menace to their country's territorial integrity but as a continuing insult to their national pride, as well as a disturbing reminder that their mission of national salvation and rejuvenation remains to be completely fulfilled.

Considering full sovereignty in all these cases a question of "great right and great wrong," the Chinese, instead of inclining to compromise on the matter, are apt to become all the more infuriated by attempts to detach any of these territories from their country. If so, they are likely to rally more closely behind the elite that can give them effective leadership in resisting foreign attempts at China's dismemberment.

In other words, foreign designs to strip China of Sinkiang, Taiwan or Tibet or all of them, even if forcibly implemented, are bound to add fuel to an already raging fire of nationalism, and are certain to provide the Communist elite with a convenient tool for exhorting the Chinese to make more sacrifices and efforts required for internal development as well as for preserving the nation's territorial integrity and political independence. It goes without saying that any such foreign designs would dash the much cherished hope that with the passage of time and, particularly, with the replacement of the present leaders in Peking by men of a younger generation, mainland China might gradually lose its revolutionary militancy in general and its hostility to "imperialist powers" in particular.

The determination to safeguard territorial integrity and political independence does not mean that Peking will always take drastic measures against foreign trespassers without regard to consequences. Patience, prudence and shrewd alternation of tactics have been as characteristic of China's approach to such problems as has determination. Perhaps this was most clearly demonstrated by Peking's decision in March 1969 to meet Soviet armed "intrusion" into the Chenpao Island [located on the Sino-Soviet border in the Ussuri River] with armed resistance, and by its subsequent readiness to hold negotiations with Moscow on border problems following Premier Kosygin's talks with Premier Chou En-lai in Peking. . . .

In the case of Taiwan, while the leaders in Peking obviously realize that the above-mentioned American and Japanese maneuvers in regard to that island, if unchecked, may complicate matters, they seem to be quite confident that time is on their side and that sooner or later any one of the following developments or a combination of them will help bring Taiwan under their control:

   1. Their own military strength will become sufficiently strong to challenge the American military umbrella over Taiwan.

2. The mainland will take such giant strides toward industrialization and general economic prosperity that its magnetism will be too strong for the political dissidents on Taiwan to resist any longer.

3. The authorities on Taiwan will become totally disenchanted with Washington and Tokyo and will believe that their best resource is to reach an understanding with Peking.

4. Washington will reach the conclusion that Taiwan's strategic importance to the United States does not, after all, justify the assumption of risks attendant to the defense of the island.

5. Washington will come to the point of view, as President Nixon may very well have, that for global strategic considerations it is more desirable to seek a *détente* with Peking than to infuriate it continuously over Taiwan. Taiwan's detachment from the mainland does not significantly reduce China's potential to become an increasingly important factor in world politics.

Peking's determination to safeguard her territorial integrity and political independence has not involved any territorial expansion at the expense of her small neighbors, contrary to a widely held popular assumption. Militant practitioners of Marxism-Leninism and implacable foes of human exploitation in all forms, the present Chinese leaders appear to be genuinely sincere when they continuously admonish their countrymen to guard against "big nation chauvinism."

The Sino-Indian military conflict in October 1962 has often been treated in the Western world as a Chinese act of aggression. The incident, however, was due mainly to conflicting claims over long sections of disputed territory along the Himalayan border between the two countries. The immediate cause of the conflict seemed to be China's determination to assert her right to maintain a recently constructed highway in the Aksai Chin area (in the western sector of the disputed territory), to expel the Indian troops which from 1959 on had penetrated into areas north of the controversial MacMahon line in the eastern sector of the disputed territory, and to forestall a much-publicized Indian general offensive to clear Chinese troops from the disputed territory. In any event, as soon as the Indian army along the border had been routed, Peking promptly announced three proposals to end the military conflict, reopen negotiations, and settle the boundary question peacefully. This was followed up by the unilateral declaration of a cease-fire, the voluntary withdrawal of troops from the areas into which the Chinese troops had newly advanced, the voluntary release of captured Indian personnel, and the return to India of large stores of military equipment. These measures effectively brought the armed conflict to a speedy conclusion.

Nor is it feasible for the Communist Chinese to encroach upon their small neighbors; any such attempt would probably prompt the intended victim to seek help from Washington or Moscow or both, whose influence in Asia Peking has sought to reduce. If an intended victim is led by a revolutionary elite, as in Vietnam, then any adventurist Chinese leader would have to ask himself whether, even in the absence of direct intervention by any of the superpowers, his country can fare any better in attempting to subdue that small country than the far more powerful and far more affluent America has been able to do in Indochina in recent years.

Defensive Mentality

Expansion beyond the traditional territorial limits also has few roots in Chinese history. Since the Ch'in (221-207 B.C.) and Han (206 B.C.-220 A.D.) dynasties the Chinese have seldom given any serious thought to the idea of pushing their frontiers beyond—roughly—their present boundaries. To be sure, China from time to time established tributary relations with such countries as Korea, Vietnam and Nepal, but her authority over those nations was more symbolic than real. In the absence of economic exploitation and political oppression, the tributary relations mainly served to guarantee peace between China on the one hand and the tributary states on the other. Throughout the centuries China remained a self-sufficient and self-sustained nation with an essentially defensive mentality, which was epitomized in the construction and periodical repairing of the Great Wall as well as in her unwillingness in the fifteenth century to use her then unrivaled naval power to seize territories in Southeast Asia and on the east African coast to which her mighty fleets made seven expeditions from 1405 to 1433. Needless to say, this conduct was in sharp contrast to the subsequent European expansion, which, among other things, was rooted in the European people's quest for trade opportunities, their missionary zeal and their interest in geographical explorations, all of which were alien to the Chinese.

The absence of territorial designs, however, does not preclude the desire to see that her small neighbors are not used by her principal antagonists against herself. Peking's policy of resolutely supporting Hanoi and other revolutionary forces in Indochina apparently has been prompted partly by this desire. So must have been the decision to send "volunteers" to Korea in late 1950. In recent years Peking has made the elimination of American influence (and, to a lesser extent, Soviet influence) from her immediate neighbors one of the most urgent tasks. In order to accomplish this task, Peking has endeavored to assure many of these countries of its reasonableness and good-neighborly intent. In April 1954 it proclaimed the now famous "five principles of peaceful coexistence" as the basic policy toward countries having different social systems. At the Bandung Conference [held in Indonesia] in April 1955 Premier Chou En-lai successfully convinced many of the assembled Afro-Asian leaders of his government's sincerity in pursuing this policy. Since the later 1950s Peking has supplemented its declarations of good-neighborly intent by signing treaties of friendship, nonaggression and/or boundary demarcation with Afghanistan, Pakistan, Nepal, Burma, Cambodia and Outer Mongolia. So far this policy has been effective in making some of the neighboring countries less fearful of Peking and in persuading them to refuse to permit the United States to use their military bases for "encircling" China.

Peking, however, has not felt obliged to observe the five principles of peaceful coexistence in its dealings with some neighboring countries whose ruling elites are hostile to China and collaborate with major "imperialist" powers, especially "US imperialism." Thailand is a case in point. Nor has Peking ever shown a want of resolution in chastising an erstwhile friendly neighbor which has begun to develop relations with China's principal adversaries that are inimical to her. Peking's hostility toward Rangoon [Burma] from the summer of 1967 to the summer of 1971 typified this behavior. What the Rangoon government actually did to draw Chinese verbal attacks on the Ne Win regime in 1967 and thereafter, and in the meantime cause Peking to make open declarations of support for the White Flag guerrillas in Burma, consisted of Ne Win's attempts to move away from Burma's earlier "neutral" position to a policy of strengthening ties with Washington, Moscow and New Delhi. . . . That it was indeed these Burmese actions, not any Chinese premeditation, that turned Peking against Rangoon after years of *paukpaw* (kinfolk) relationship has been made unmistakably clear by the recently achieved *détente* between the two capitals, which came on the heels of the virtual termination of the US aid program in Burma and the departure from that country on June 30, 1971, of the last contingent of the American Military Equipment Delivery Team.

Dangerous Ambitions

In the case of Japan, not only has Tokyo aroused Peking's ire by allying itself with Washington since the early 1950s, but Japanese ambitions and capabilities have caused Peking to fear that if the hands of "the Japanese reactionaries" are not stayed in time, Tokyo—even in the absence of American encouragement and support—will pose an increasingly grave threat to her neighbors in Asia, including China. In addition to Tokyo's "designs with regard to Taiwan," other ambitions and activities of "the Japanese reactionaries" that have been disquieting to Peking are their assiduous efforts to revive the Bushido spirit of the Japanese people [chivalric code of the Samurai of feudal Japan, emphasizing loyalty and courage and preferring death to dishonor], their ever expanding programs of rearmament, their growing capabilities and desire for manufacturing nuclear weapons, their diplomatic flirtations with Moscow, their economic penetration into South Korea and many Southeast Asian countries and, above all, their "dream" of recreating "the Great Asia Co-Prosperity Sphere." However, Peking's enmity toward "the Japanese reactionaries" does not imply a hatred of the Japanese people in general. As in the case of all the other countries whose governments have not been friendly to the new China, Peking has always made a distinction between the people of a country and their government. Moreover, even a profound distrust of the present Japanese government has not tempted Peking to promote a Communist revolution in Japan, which it does not deem realistic. Rather, Peking seems to believe that, as of now, the best hope lies in the waging of a joint struggle with all the Japanese political parties and groups that are opposed to the revival of Japanese militarism and aggression. Meanwhile, Peking has been doing its best to arouse general international vigilance against Tokyo's "dangerous ambitions."

A major objective of Maoist leadership is to restore China to a respectable place in the family of nations. Conscious of the country's past greatness and incensed by the humiliation that she has suffered in modern times at the hands of Western powers and Japan, Mao and his associates have taken this task most seriously. On September 21, 1949, Mao declared . . . "Our nation will never be insulted again. We have stood up." In keeping with the spirit of this statement, the

Peking regime let it be known at its inception that the new China would establish diplomatic relations with only those countries that would treat her on the basis of equality and friendliness and had severed relations with "the Kuomintang [i.e. Nationalist] reactionaries"; rather than automatically abide by the treaties and agreements concluded between the Kuomintang and foreign governments, she would "recognize, abrogate, revise, or renegotiate them according to their respective contents." Not a few of the existing treaties and agreements contained provisions injurious to Chinese interests and undermining Chinese pride.

Ousting the West

Indicative of the early determination of the Peking regime to rid China of all lingering legacies of foreign domination and exploitation were the expropriation of Western business firms in China; the seizure of Western military barracks in the former legation headquarters in Peking; the closing down of foreign-owned newspapers and other publications; the termination of the control by foreign missionaries of Catholic and Protestant churches; the efforts to "deflate the arrogance" of those Western diplomats, businessmen, and missionaries who had been accustomed to "riding roughshod" over China; and the shelling of the British gunboat Amethyst on the Yangtze River on April 20-21, 1949. This last step not only quickly forced England to give up its residual right to sail naval vessels on Chinese inland waterways but also dramatized the new China's boldness in defending her national interest and dignity.

In the meantime, Peking's quest for a respectable place in the family of nations manifested itself in its repeated vows not to tolerate any foreign interference with China's internal affairs (including the question of Taiwan) and in its determination to develop nuclear weapons and make space explorations. That Peking's primary objective in developing nuclear weapons is to enhance her international prestige and to neutralize the same weapons possessed by her potential adversaries was attested to by Foreign Minister Ch'en I in 1962 when he was quoted as having said: ". . . We are likewise working to develop an atomic bomb of our own for the sole reason that the capitalists consider us underdeveloped and defenseless as long as we lack the ultimate weapon." In addition, since she began testing nuclear weapons in 1964, Peking has repeatedly reaffirmed the essentially defensive nature of her nuclear policy by reiterating that she will never be the first to use nuclear weapons in a war.

In the late 1950s the quest for major-nation status, coupled with other issues, prompted Peking to refuse to "crawl to the baton of the Soviet leaders," to espouse "complete equality" for the "Socialist states" and the Communist and workers' parties, and to emphasize the policy of self-reliance for economic development and national defense, lest reliance on foreign assistance lead to foreign domination or at least foreign derision such as Peking had experienced in its relations with Moscow. Peking's determination to establish itself as a major power in the world is reflected in the policy of refusing to abide by any international agreement that has been concluded without her consent. For about a century prior to 1949 China was forced to accede to many international agreements against her wishes and much to her detriment. While admission to the United Nations was deemed likely to enhance her prestige, the Peking government did not regard membership in that body as an indispensable symbol of international respectability if it was to be attained at the risk of prejudicing the claim over Taiwan. Thus it insisted on the expulsion of the Nationalist delegation from that body and the absence, in the UN resolution admitting Peking's delegation, of any reference "to the effect that the status of Taiwan remains to be determined." The General Assembly's adoption of the Albanian Resolution on October 25, 1971, reflected the international community's realization that Peking indeed would not join the United Nations under any other circumstances.

China's Principal Enemy

Still another external goal is to change the status quo of the nations of the world. This is aimed not only at "assisting the oppressed and exploited peoples to deliver themselves from the yoke of imperialism, colonialism, neocolonialism," but also at reducing the strength of "the imperialists and colonialists," especially the United States, which the leaders in Peking regard as China's principal enemy on the following grounds: it once assisted the Kuomintang during the last phase of the Chinese civil war on the mainland; has been hostile to the new China; occupies Taiwan, Quemoy and Matsu by means of supporting the Chiang Kai-shek regime in Taipei; asserts that the status of Taiwan has not been settled; plots to detach Taiwan permanently from the mainland; thwarts Peking's efforts to reassert China's legitimate claims as a major power; encircles China with a cordon of military bases; intrudes into Chinese air space and territorial waters with airplanes and warships; threatens China's southern frontier with its invasion of the Indochinese states; colludes with the Soviet revisionists and the "reactionaries" in New Delhi, Tokyo and elsewhere for an anti-China holy alliance; and stands in the way of the world Communist movement. One of Peking's major strategies for effecting a total alteration of the status quo in the world is to organize an international united front against imperialism, colonialism and neocolonialism. Such a united front is deemed feasible because Peking perceives "an inexorably anti-imperialist current in the Afro-Asian countries as well as in Latin America." While admitting that victories of great historic significance have already been won by the national liberation movements in Asia, Africa and Latin America, the Communist Chinese, unlike many Western and Soviet leaders, contend that imperialism, colonialism and neocolonialism remain "the most ferocious enemies" of the peoples in those regions and that the struggles against these "enemies" will continue to surge ahead rather than recede.

To form a united front with the peoples in Asia, Africa and Latin America, Peking believes, would not only be an effective way of fighting imperialism, colonialism and neocolonialism as it may force their enemies, especially "US imperialism," to disperse their strength and thus lessen pressure on China, but it may also facilitate the overthrow of capitalism in North America and Western Europe and hasten the victory of the world Communist movement. This belief is based on the Leninist theory that the colonies and semicolonies in Asia, Africa and Latin America constitute the rear of the capitalist world (as the latter's sources of raw materials and outlets for manufactured goods and surplus capital) and that if the capitalist world has been stripped of its rear, then it can be easily toppled. . . . To Peking, only after such a [united] front has come into existence and has successfully carried out the more urgent and crucial task of defeating colonialism, neocolonialism and imperialism can it fulfill the mission of hastening the victory of the international proletarian revolution. On the other hand, active support to local Communists in the neutralist countries, if given at this stage of the struggle, is thought likely to hinder the formation and maintenance of the proposed united front —for it will alarm and alienate the nationalist governments of the neutralist countries at a time when the local Communists, if any, are still too weak to take over the reins of their respective states. . . .

Two Intermediate Zones

Although the policy of organizing an international united front thus far remains more a vision than a reality, Peking's flexibility and patience in dealing with the emerging nations and its self-projected image as the champion against the injustices and inequities of the status quo have enabled it to develop friendly or at least polite relations with more than thirty non-Communist countries in Asia, Africa and Latin America. More significantly, many of these countries have publicly endorsed Peking's position on some international problems of utmost importance to China. The official statements made by many Afro-Asian countries that Taiwan should be returned to China is of particular importance in terms of Sino-American and Sino-Japanese relations. Those statements, if consistently adhered to, might make it difficult, if not impossible, for Washington's (and also Tokyo's) "two Chinas" policy or "one China and one Taiwan" policy to find sufficient international approval to be maintained.

Recognizing the wisdom of uniting with all that can be united in the struggle against the principal enemy and being aware of the developing schisms in NATO and other US-led alliances, Peking since 1964 has broadened the scope of the proposed united front by advancing the concept of "two intermediate zones" and by stressing the urgency of "opposing the US imperialist venture to dominate the world." According to this concept, there is a vast intermediate area between the United States and the Soviet Union "whose leaders are now colluding with US imperialism for world domination." The intermediate zone is composed of two parts: One part consists of the independent countries and those striving for independence in Asia, Africa and Latin America; it is called the first intermediate zone. The second part consists of the whole of Western Europe, Oceania, Canada and other capitalist countries and is called the second intermediate zone. Countries in this second intermediate zone are said to have a dual character:

> While their ruling classes are exploiters and oppressors, these countries themselves are subjected to US control, interference, and bullying. They therefore try their best to free themselves from US control. In this regard, they have something in common with the Socialist countries and the peoples of various countries.

One of the preliminary steps taken by Peking to bring about the envisaged grand alliance of the two intermediate zones was its establishment of diplomatic relations with France in January 1964. Peking's recent expression of approval of the admission of Britain and three other countries into the Common Market was also in line with this policy: As the Chinese saw it, an enlarged and deepened economic community in Western Europe would "constitute a serious obstacle to the United States and the Soviet Union in pushing their policies for hegemony in Europe." A further development of the same policy was Peking's diplomatic initiatives toward Eastern Europe. Since the Soviet invasion of Czechoslovakia in 1968 and the subsequent "fabrication" of the Brezhnev Doctrine which asserts that Moscow has the right to take military action against any Socialist country in the interest of the security of the Socialist community as a whole, Peking has seen both a need and an opportunity to seek the cooperation of as many Eastern European countries as possible in thwarting "the Soviet socioimperialists' rapacious expansionist ambitions." Such cooperation is deemed necessary because it would have the direct effect of disrupting the Soviet Union's western flank and the indirect effect of limiting its freedom of action vis-à-vis China. As for the opportunity to secure such cooperation, Peking finds its existence in the Eastern European people's covert and overt resistance to Soviet "domination," "plunder," and "intimidations."

Out of these considerations Peking now has strengthened its influence in the Balkans, first of all, by supplementing its long-standing alliance with Tirana [Albania] with the development of increasingly closer ties with Bucharest [Rumania]. Since 1969 there also has been a slow but significant improvement in relations with Belgrade [Yugoslavia], which for the preceding ten years had been a target of bitter Chinese attacks for its "revisionism" and its "traitorous" ties with the West. . . .

Nixon's Journey

If the preceding analysis of Peking's intentions and behavior is basically correct, then it is only logical to draw the following inferences in regard to President Nixon's . . . journey to Peking. First, given Peking's essentially defensive posture in world affairs, the self-sufficient and self-sustained nature of its economy, its preoccupation with internal transformation on all fronts, and the Chinese people's traditional inward-looking mentality, there are, in fact, no irreconcilable conflicts of interest between the United States and China that foredoom the President's quest for a *détente* with the Chinese leaders—provided that his overtures to them take full cognizance of their acute concern for China's security and their unshakable determination to preserve their country's territorial integrity, political sovereignty and national dignity.

Judging by their demonstrated patience, sophistication, and ability to foresake "narrow tactical gains" in the interest of "long-range purposes," the present leaders in Peking, on their part, can be expected to reciprocate such American cognizance of their paramount interests by showing a willingness to resolve such outstanding issues as the future of Taiwan and the withdrawal of American military forces from Indochina in a manner and at a pace that would not be detrimental to the vital interests and national honor of both countries.

Second, in view of the mutual concern about the intentions and growing power of the Soviet Union and Japan, the Chinese leaders are likely to show interest in any American proposal aimed at developing a "multipolar diplomacy" in the world that would give Washington, Peking and other major powers more options in safeguarding their national security and economic interests. However, it would be wrong to assume that Peking's willingness to exchange views with President Nixon on questions of concern to the two sides stems primarily from the desire to seek American help in checking Moscow and Tokyo. While any American cooperation in restraining Soviet "ambitions" and Japanese "militarism" would be helpful, the Maoist leadership, which has been profoundly disillusioned by their erstwhile Soviet ally, certainly will not abandon self-reliance as the principal way of achieving national security (as well as economic development) in favor of a new foreign promise of aid. Thus any hope that Peking may soften its basic position in regard to Taiwan and the American military presence in Indochina in exchange for some form of American cooperation or even sheer American neutrality in Sino-Soviet and Sino-Japanese relations is unrealistic, especially when a large-scale military confrontation with Moscow and Tokyo is neither imminent nor inevitable.

Agreement Likely?

With regard to the control or limitation of nuclear and other strategic weapons, President Nixon can avoid an unnecessary disappointment during his stay in Peking if he realizes in advance that at least in the foreseeable future China will not accede to an international agreement that would permit her actual and potential foes to retain their nuclear and missile superiority while inhibiting her from improving her capabilities in those vital fields. The Chinese position will not change as long as she continues to be inferior in those fields; as long as she lacks a convincing guarantee from the more advanced nuclear and missile powers that they will never use nuclear and missile weapons in a war against her; and as long as she has no compelling reasons to "cease and desist" in experimentation with and manufacturing of nuclear weapons and missiles. However, if in the future Peking ever concludes that particular arrangements will better serve its interests, the Chinese government will be as willing to accept such arrangements as would any other nation that has reached the same conclusion.

Finally, although China is unlikely to mute, in the foreseeable future, her revolutionary propaganda regardless of the results of President Nixon's . . . trip to Peking, any announced or even secret understanding that the President may reach with his Chinese hosts on some of the major issues that have estranged the two countries for so long is bound to go a long way toward soothing China's long-held sense of grievances against "imperialism," which more than anything else has been the main cause of the new China's "intransigence" since 1949. If so, then in time even Peking's propaganda against the status quo in the world may gradually lose its intensity, if not come to a complete stop.

BIBLIOGRAPHY

An asterisk (*) preceding a reference indicates that the article or a part of it has been reprinted in this book.

BOOKS, PAMPHLETS, AND DOCUMENTS

*Barnett, A. D. China after Mao; with selected documents. Princeton University Press. '67.
> *Reprinted in this book*: Decision of the Chinese Communist party concerning the cultural revolution. p 263-76.

Barnett, A. D. China on the eve of Communist takeover. Praeger. '63.

Barnett, A. D. Communist China; the early years, 1949-55. Praeger. '64.

Barnett, A. D. Our China policy; the need for change. (Headline Series no 204) Foreign Policy Association. 345 E. 46th St. New York 10017. '71.

Barnett, A. D. and Reischauer, E. O. eds. The United States and China; the next decade. Praeger. '70.

Buck, P. S. China as I see it; comp. & ed. by Theodore F. Harris. John Day. '70.

Bueler, W. M. U. S. China policy and the problem of Taiwan. Colorado Associated University Press. 1424 15th St. Boulder, Colo. 80302. '71.

Chen, Kuan-I, and Uppal, J. S. comps. Comparative development of India and China. Free Press. '71.
> *Title on spine*: India and China.

Chen, Lung-chu and Lasswell, H. D. Formosa, China, and the United Nations; Formosa in the world community. St. Martin's. '67.

Clubb, O. E. 20th century China. Columbia University Press. '64.

Croizier, R. C. ed. China's cultural legacy and communism. Praeger. '70.

Durdin, Tillman and others. The New York Times report from Red China. Quadrangle. '71.

Fairbank, J. K. China: the people's Middle kingdom and the U.S.A. Harvard University Press. '67.

Fairbank, J. K. The United States and China. Harvard University Press. '71.

Feis, Herbert. The China tangle: The American effort in China from Pearl Harbor to the Marshall mission. Atheneum. '65.

Fessler, Loren. China; by [the author] and the editors of Life. Time. '63.

*Foreign Policy Association. Great Decisions 1972. The Association. 345 E. 46th St. New York 10017. '72.
    Reprinted in this book: Excerpts from Fact Sheet no 7, Our China policy. p 49-59.

Gasster, Michael. China's struggle to modernize. Knopf. '72.

Gittings, John. The role of the Chinese army. Oxford. '67.
    Issued under the auspices of the Royal institute of international affairs.

Goldston, Robert. The rise of Red China. Bobbs. '67.

Greene, Felix. Awakened China: the country Americans don't know. Doubleday. '61.

Greene, Fred. U. S. policy and the security of Asia. (Council on Foreign Relations. The U.S. and China in world affairs) McGraw. '68.

Grey, Anthony. Hostage in Peking. Joseph, M. '70.

Guillermaz, Jacques. A history of the Chinese Communist party; tr. by Anne Destenay. Random House. '72.

Halperin, M. H. China and the bomb; written under the auspices of the Center for International Affairs and the East Asian Research Center, Harvard University. Praeger. '65.

Hobbs, Lisa. I saw Red China. McGraw. '66.

Hunter, Neale. Shanghai journal; an eyewitness account of the Cultural Revolution. Praeger. '69.

Johnson, C. E. Communist China & Latin America, 1959-1967. Columbia University Press. '70.
    Review. Problems of Communism. 20:72-6. My. '71. Moscow and Peking in Latin America. Y. H. Ferguson.

Koningsberger, Hans. Love and hate in China. McGraw. '67.

*League of Women Voters. The Cultural Revolution: its zigs and zags. '68.

Lewis, J. W. ed. The city in Communist China. Stanford University Press. '71.

Macciocchi, M. A. Daily life in revolutionary China. Monthly Review Press. '72.

Maxwell, N. G. A. India's China war. Cape, J. '70.

Mehnert, Klaus. China returns [tr. from German]. Dutton. '72.

Moorsteen, R. H. and Abramowitz, Morton. Remaking China policy; U.S.-China relations and governmental decision-making. Harvard University Press. '71.

Myrdal, Jan. Report from a Chinese village. Pantheon. '65.

Myrdal, Jan and Kessle, Gun. China: the revolution continued. Pantheon. '70.

Newman, Joseph, ed. A new look at Red China. U.S. News & World Report, Inc, 2300 N St. N.W. Washington, D.C. 20037. '71.

*Oksenberg, Michel. China: the convulsive society. (Headline Series no 203) Foreign Policy Association, 345 E. 46th St. New York 10017. '70.

Pye, L. W. The spirit of Chinese politics; a psychocultural study of the authority crisis in political development. MIT Press. '68.

Rice, E. E. Mao's way. University of California. '72.

Robottom, John. China in revolution. McGraw. '69.

Roy, Jules. Journey through China; tr. from the French by Francis Price. Harper. '67.

Rowland, John. A history of Sino-Indian relations; hostile co-existence. Van Nostrand. '67.

✓Salisbury, H. E. Orbit of China. Harper. '67.

Schram, S. R. ed. The political thought of Mao Tse-tung. rev. & enl. ed. Praeger. '69.

Schwartz, B. I. Communism and China; ideology in flux. Harvard University Press. '68.

Shabad, Theodore. China's changing map; national and regional development, 1949-71. Praeger. '72.

Snow, Edgar. The long revolution. Random House. '72.

Snow, Edgar. Red China today; rev. and updated ed. of The other side of the river. Random House. '71.

Snow, L. W. China on stage: an American actress in the People's Republic. Random House. '72.

Stoessinger, J. G. Nations in darkness: China, Russia, and America. Random House. '71.

Terrill, Ross. 800,000,000: The real China. Little. '72.
    Excerpts. Atlantic. 228:90-6+. N. '71; 229:39-54+. Ja. '72.

Topping, Seymour. Journey between two Chinas. Harper. '72.

Van Ness, Peter. Revolution and Chinese foreign policy: Peking's support for wars of national liberation. University of California. '71.

Wheelwright, E. L. and McFarlane, B. J. The Chinese road to socialism; economics of the cultural revolution. Monthly Review Press. '70.

Wilson, R. G. Anatomy of China: an introduction to one quarter of mankind. Weybright & Talley. '68.

Wolf, Margery. The house of Lim: a study of a Chinese farm family. Appleton. '68.

Zagoria, D. S. The Sino-Soviet conflict, 1956-1961. Princeton University Press. '62.

PERIODICALS

America. 120:280-1. Mr. 8, '69. Red China in Europe. David Bligh.

America. 121:87-90. Ag. 16, '69. China: a positive policy. W. V. Kennedy.

America. 125:87-8. Ag. 21, '71. China as it is today. Louis La Dany.

America. 125:359. N. 6, '71. Mao wipes the slate clean.

America. 126:314-17, 418-23. Mr. 25, Ap. 22, '72. Religion in Communist China. J. C. Haughey.

Asian Affairs. 58:274-83. O. '71. China: a background. David Wilson.

Asian Outlook. 6:12-18. O. '71. An analysis of intensified Chinese Communist diplomatic activity. Chiang Tao.

Asian Survey. 11:629-44. Jl. '71. China's cautious relations with North Korea and Indochina. R. R. Simmons.

Atlantic. 222:14-17. Ag. '68. Report; impact of the cultural revolution. A. C. Miller.

Atlantic. 227:12+. Ja. '71. China policy. J. A. Cohen.

Atlas. 20:43. Jl. '71. Why is China supporting West Pakistan?

Bulletin of the Atomic Scientists. 25:2-88. F. '69. China after the Cultural Revolution; symposium.

*Bulletin of the Atomic Scientists. 28:15-21. F. '72. Chinese foreign policy in perspective. F. W. Houn.

Bulletin of the Atomic Scientists. 28:28-35. Ja. '72. Mainland China's evolving nuclear deterrent. C. H. Murphy.

Business Week. p 76-8+. Jl. 15, '67. Havoc that Mao has wrought.

Business Week. p 46-7. Jl. 24, '71. Red China: the economy behind the open door.

Business Week. p 85. O. 30, '71. What the tourists are finding in mainland China.

Catholic World. 213:259-60. S. '71. Nixon visit and religion in China. J. B. Sheerin.

China Quarterly. p 245-73. Ap./Je. '71. Small industry and the Chinese model of development. Carl Riskin.

Christian Century. 87:926. Jl. 29, '70. China; Maoist economic development. Hwa Yu.

Christian Century. 88:1278. O. 27, '71. China: normalizing of relations with the nations and peoples of the world. Hwa Yu.

Christian Century. 89:234. F. 23, '72. China: quality of life. Hwa Yu.

Commonweal. 85:553-5. F. 17, '67. Will China intervene? the stakes in Vietnam. W. C. McWilliams.

Comparative Politics. 3:323-60. Ap. '71. Policy making under Mao Tse-tung, 1949-1968. M. C. Oksenberg.

Contemporary Review. 218:250-4. My. '71. China's population. V. D'Alton.

Contemporary Review. 219:155-60. S. '71. Chinese diplomacy and the United Nations. Robert Boardman.

Current. 108:61-4. Je. '69. Shifting great power politics; the end of U.S.-Soviet hegemony.

Current. 117:56-61. Ap. '70. Thaw in U.S.-Chinese relations? O. E. Clubb.

Current. 130:3-14. Je. '71. Dealing with China; symposium.
Selections by Pearl S. Buck and others.

Current History. 51:134-9+. S. '66. Peking's Cultural Revolution. S. Y. Dai.

Current History. 55:129-70+. S. '68. Mainland China; symposium.

Current History. 57:129-74+. S. '69. Communist China after twenty years; symposium.

Current History. 59:129-69+. S. '70. Mainland China, 1970; symposium.

Current History. 61:129-76+. S. '71. Communist China, 1971; symposium.

Current History. 61:210-14+. O. '71. Sino-Soviet relations: the view from Moscow. J. R. Thomas.

Economist. 238:47-8. Mr. 27, '71. Republicans on the road to Peking.

Economist. 241:13-15. O. 30, '71. The Chinese are coming in.

Far Eastern Economic Review. 66:639-42. D. 18, '69. China's economy: great leaps and club feet. L. F. Goodstadt.

Far Eastern Economic Review. 72:21-3. Ap. 10, '71. Might and right (status of China-Soviet Union relations). L. F. Goodstadt.

Far Eastern Economic Review. 75:5-7. Mr. 4, '72. For Asia, the promise of better days—if the big powers behave. L. F. Goodstadt.

Far Eastern Economic Review. 75:7-13. Mr. 11, '72. China: death of a revolution.

Foreign Affairs. 45:246-59. Ja. '67. China convulsed. Mark Gayn.

Foreign Affairs. 45:683-93. Jl. '67. Tension on the Sino-Soviet border. C. P. Fitzgerald.

Foreign Affairs. 46:137-50. O. '67. China's next phase. R. S. Elegant.

Foreign Affairs. 47:449-63. Ap. '69. China's foreign policy in historical perspective. J. K. Fairbank.

Foreign Affairs. 48:427-42. Ap. '70. Nuclear China and U.S. arms policy. A. D. Barnett.

Foreign Affairs. 48:701-11. Jl. '70. China: period of suspense. Louis La Dany.

Foreign Affairs. 49:201-17. Ja. '71. Nixon doctrine and our Asian commitments. E. C. Ravenal.

Foreign Affairs. 49:381-94. Ap. '71. Image and reality in Indochina. H. E. Salisbury.

Foreign Affairs. 50:30-43. O. '71. Recognizing China. J. A. Cohen.

Foreign Affairs. 50:444-58. Ap. '72. China and Taiwan: the economic issues. R. W. Barnett.

Foreign Policy. 5:88-106. Winter '71-'72. Is there a China market? D. H. Perkins.

Fortune. 74:134-9+. N. '66. Red China's sinking revolution. C. J. V. Murphy.

Fortune. 86:110-17+. Ag. '72. I have seen China—and they work. Louis Kraar.

International Affairs. 47:31-44. Ja. '71. Threat from China. Neville Maxwell.

International Affairs. 47:45-62. Ja. '71. China after Mao. D. M. Ray.

Library Journal. 97:2341-7. Jl. '72. Sixty good books on China; a basic collection for the general reader. C. W. Hayford and A. J. Nathan.

Life. 60:26-35. Ap. 8, '66. Red romance that went sour [with reports].

Life. 70:44. Mr. 12, '71. We need a new Asia policy.

Life. 70:46-8. Ap. 30, '71. Conversation with Mao Tse-tung. Edgar Snow.

Life. 72:46-7+. Mr. 17, '72. Journey back to another China. T. H. White.

Look. 30:25-8. Ag. 23, '66. Hidden battle for power in Red China. Victor Zorza.

Look. 34:19-26. F. 10, '70. New look into Mao's China. Jan Myrdal.

*Modern Age. 16:130-45. Spring '72. Peking and Moscow: the permanence of conflict. S. T. Possony.

Nation. 204:326-9. Mr. 13, '67. China puzzle: old man in a hurry. C. P. Fitzgerald.

Nation. 205:325-8. O. 9, '67. Mao's Cultural Revolution. C. P. Fitzgerald.

Nation. 211:293-5. O. 5, '70. Passing the buck to Tokyo. Albert Axelbank.

Nation. 212:305-8. Mr. 8, '71. With Sihanouk in Peking; interview, ed. by Alessandro Casella. Norodem Sihanouk.

Nation. 213:67-8. Ag. 2, '71. Protestant ethic, Chinese style.

*Nation. 213:361-7. O. 18, '71. "Beckoning a new generation." Roland Berger.

Nation. 214:194-5. F. 14, '72. Peking talks.

Nation. 214:230-3. F. 21, '72. Table in Peking: History writes the agenda. Melvin Gurtov.

National Geographic. 140:800-33. D. '71. Return to changing China. Audrey Topping.

National Review. 23:741-2. Jl. 13, '71. Newthink.

National Review. 24:210. Mr. 3, '72. What quid for what quo? James Burnham.

National Review. 24:465. Ap. 28, '72. Hong Kong and Red China. E. M. von Kuehnelt-Leddihn.

Natural History. 79:52-6. Ja. '70. Chinese peoples. I. B. Taeuber.

New Leader. 54:9-11. N. 29, '71. China bids for Africa: a suitor amid chaperons. R. W. Howe.

New Republic. 155:14-15. O. 8, '66. Why the Red Guards? explanations of the Chinese crisis. Victor Zorza.

New Republic. 155:16-20. O. 29, '66. China and Vietnam. Ross Terrill.

New Republic. 164:18-20. Ap. 3, '71. That Chinese threat; adaptation of address. A. S. Whiting.

New Republic. 164:18-21. Ap. 10, '71. Aftermath of the Cultural Revolution. Edgar Snow.

New Republic. 164:20-3. My. 1, '71. Population care and control. Edgar Snow.

New Republic. 164:9-12. My. 22, '71. Army and the party. Edgar Snow.

New Republic. 165:17-19. Jl. 10, '71. Negotiating with China. A. S. Whiting.

New Republic. 166:4. F. 26, '72. TRB from Washington: American revisionism.

New Republic. 166:11-15. F. 26, '72. China observed; excerpts from reports. Edgar Snow.

New York Times. p 15. F. 23, '72. Facts about China's people and long history.

New York Times. p 16. F. 23, '72. China since 1949: seeking the road to national greatness. O. E. Clubb.

*New York Times. p 16. F. 28, '72. Text of U.S.-Chinese communiqué.

New York Times. p 1+. Jl. 23, '72. Peking document details anti-Mao plot. Bernard Gwertzman.

*New York Times. p 1+. Jl. 25, '72. Shift in strategy by Peking is seen. William Beecher.

New York Times. p 35. Ag. 2, '72. A gentle breeze from China. C. L. Sulzberger.

New York Times. p 38. Ag. 29, '72. For the gifted of China, schools called palaces. John Burns.

New York Times. S. 4, 6-9. '72. Articles on China. B. W. Tuchman.

New York Times. p 5. S. 6, '72. Moscow accuses China on Lin Piao. Hedrick Smith.

New York Times. p 1+. S. 14, '72. Mainland China reported buying first U.S. wheat. E. W. Kenworthy.

New York Times. p 3. S. 25, '72. China restoring exams in her schools. John Burns.

New York Times Magazine. p 22-3+. My. 1, '66. China's crisis of foreign policy. D. S. Zagoria.

New York Times Magazine. p 30-1+. My. 22, '66. Why Peking casts us as the villain. J. K. Fairbank.

New York Times Magazine. p 26-7+. Ag. 28, '66. Through darkest Red China. A. R. Topping.

New York Times Magazine. p 28-9+. Ap. 21, '68. Who's afraid of the domino theory? D. S. Zagoria.
    Reply with rejoinder: p 22+. My. 12, '68. J. E. McSherry.

New York Times Magazine. p 10-11+. Jl. 27, '69. Urgent question that dominates the Asian heartland today is: Will there be war between Russia and China? H. E. Salisbury.

New York Times Magazine. p 36-7+. Mr. 8, '70. What makes Mao a Maoist. S. R. Schram.

New York Times Magazine. p 29+. O. 24, '71. Visit to Peking university; what the Cultural Revolution was all about. B. M. Frolic.

New York Times Magazine. p 12-13+. F. 20, '72. Mao's China, 1972: a nostalgia for Yenan, 1935. Alessandro Casella.

New Yorker. 47:115-17. My. 1, '71. Letter from Washington [Washington-Peking axis, a possibility]. R. H. Rovere.

New Yorker. 48:98+. My. 6, '72. Reporter in China. Joseph Kraft.

Newsweek. 67:35-8+. Mr. 7, '66. China: dangers of misunderstanding.

Newsweek. 69:32-9+. Ja. 30, '67. Mao and the struggle for China.

Newsweek. 75:84. Ja. 26, '70. Does China matter much? Stewart Alsop.

Newsweek. 75:58+. Ap. 20, '70. New devil figure.

Newsweek. 76:60. Ag. 31, '70. Bargains from Mao; Communist stores in Hong Kong.

Newsweek. 76:51-2. N. 16, '70. China courts the barbarians.

Newsweek. 77:33-4. F. 8, '71. China policy: time for a thaw.

Newsweek. 77:28-9. My. 3, '71. Two-China policy? views of S. T. Agnew.

Newsweek. 78:28-35. S. 13, '71. China: a sense of initiative. Marc Riboud.

Newsweek. 78:31-2. O. 4, '71. China: something must be happening.

Newsweek. 78:51-2. O. 18, '71. Round-trip ticket to Peking.

Newsweek. 78:26-7. N. 8, '71. Power struggle in Peking.

Newsweek. 78:27-8. N. 8, '71. Pleasures of victory.

Newsweek. 78:56-7. D. 20, '71. Learning about China.

*Newsweek. 79:36-9. F. 21, '72. What it means to be Chinese.

*Newsweek. 79:44-7. F. 21, '72. Coming of age in Communist China.

Newsweek. 79:24-5. Mr. 6, '72. Chinese diary. Mel Elfin.

Newsweek. 79:18-19. Mr. 13, '72. After the ball was over.

Newsweek. 79:32. Mr. 13, '72. Asia: waiting for the avalanche.

Newsweek. 79:75. Mr. 13, '72. The rocky road to China trade.

Orbis. 13:783-821. Fall '69. The Chinese Communist cauldron. S. T. Possony.

Orbis. 15:118-33. Spring '71. The Sino-Soviet relationship and the United States. H. G. Gelber.

Pacific Affairs. 44:18-38. Spring '71. Some aspects of China's Asian policy in the Cultural Revolution and its aftermath. S. W. Simon.

*Parents Magazine and Better Family Living. 47:52-3+. Ap. '72. How the oldest civilization in the world brings up its youngest members. Lisa Hobbs.

*Problems of Communism. 15:14-20. N./D. '66. A nation in agony. T. H. Chen.

Problems of Communism. 20:45-59. Ja./Ap. '71. Conflict on the Ussuri: a clash of nationalisms. H. C. Hinton.

Problems of Communism. 20:1-13. S. '71. New face of Maoist China. Tillman Durdin.
    Excerpts: Current. 133:48-64. O. '71. Achieving a new stability.

Problems of Communism. 20:1-32. N./D. '71; 21:48-70. Ja./F. '72. China's new diplomacy: a symposium.

*Problems of Communism. 21:16-24. Mr./Ap. '72. Peking's African diplomacy. G. T. Yu.

Progressive. 35:19-22. Ag. '71. China's strategic shift. O. E. Clubb.
    Excerpts. Current. 132:58-64. S. '71.

Ramparts. 10:10-19. Ag. '71. Inside China: in the wake of the Cultural Revolution. John Gittings.

Ramparts. 10:7-8+. Mr. '72. Purge in China. David Horowitz.

Ramparts. 10:7+. My. '72. Et tu China? David Kolodney.

Reader's Digest. 99:69-73. O. '71. What is behind Red China's smile? C. J. V. Murphy.

Reader's Digest. 100:241-4+. My. '72. China diary. J. A. Michener.

Saturday Review. 53:32-4. Ap. 25, '70. What worries Chairman Mao. O. E. Clubb.

Saturday Review. 54:27-30. S. 18, '71. What new role for the People's Republic of China? R. C. Hottelet.

Saturday Review. 54:36-9. O. 23, '71. All you need to know for a trip to China. L. W. Snow.

Saturday Review. 54:14-16+. D. 18, '71. If ever the twain shall meet. B. P. Clark.

Senior Scholastic. 88:14-16. Mr. 18, '66. Sino-Soviet border comrades up in arms.

Senior Scholastic. 89 pt 2:5-6. S. 23, '66. Profile of the Sino-Soviet split.

Senior Scholastic. 98:15-17. My. 10, '71. U.S. and China: new pages.

Senior Scholastic. 100:3-8. Mr. 13, '72. China and the U.S.: behind the smiles and the handshakes; questions and answers.

Seventeen. 30:142+. O. '71. Ping Pong diplomat. Judy Bochenski.

Time. 96:26. Ag. 24, '70. Army's man.

Time. 96:20+. S. 7, '70. Lights go on again.

Time. 96:36-44. N. 16, '70. China: the siege of the ants; celebrating 21st anniversary of Communist victory.

Time. 98:40. O. 18, '71. Alive and well in Peking; Mao back in sight.

*Time. 99:32-4. F. 21, '72. Life in the Middle Kingdom.

Travel. 136:66-9. Jl. '71. Curtain going up?

U.S. News & World Report. 60:38-41. F. 14, '66. How vulnerable is Red China?

U.S. News & World Report. 61:48-56. S. 12, '66. What's really going on inside China; with interviews with Hugo Portisch and Lorenz Stucki.

*U.S. News & World Report. 63:36-8. O. 2, '67. As Red China plunges deeper into chaos; impact of disorders.

U.S. News & World Report. 66:52-4. Mr. 31, '69. Red China: world's no. 1 enigma.

U.S. News & World Report. 68:52-5. Je. 22, '70. Big changes inside Red China.

U.S. News & World Report. 70:68-71. F. 15, '71. Close-up of Red China: now a real leap forward.

U.S. News & World Report. 70:14-16. My. 10, '71. Doing business with Red China: myth or reality?

U.S. News & World Report. 70:88. Je. 14, '71. What admission of Red China to the U.N. really means. David Lawrence.

U.S. News & World Report. 71:42-5. S. 20, '71. Red giants battle over Asia. J. N. Wallace.

U.S. News & World Report. 71:46-8. S. 27, '71. When Red China becomes a nuclear superpower.

U.S. News & World Report. 71:32-5. O. 18, '71. Behind the turmoil in Red China; with comments by Tillman Durdin.

U.S. News & World Report. 71:29. N. 22, '71. Clues to fight for power in Red China.

U.S. News & World Report. 72:26-7. F. 14, '72. Nixon and Chou En-lai; excerpts from interview with Neville Maxwell.

U.S. News & World Report. 72:16-18. F. 21, '72. Clues to watch for in Nixon mission.

U.S. News & World Report. 72:16-17. F. 28, '72. Second-rate power, with a long way to go; pictogram.

U.S. News & World Report. 72:18-19. Mr. 6, '72. Four-power balance unlike anything we've had in the past; interview. A. D. Barnett.

*U.S. News & World Report. 72:22-6+. Mr. 13, '72. Life is earnest, and rather grim; China revisited. R. P. Martin.

U.S. News & World Report. 72:100-2. Mr. 20, '72. Analysis: Where is China really headed under Mao. R. P. Martin.

U.S. News & World Report. 72:44-9. My. 29, '72. Inside Red China today; interviews. M. J. Mansfield; Hugh Scott.

UNESCO Courier. 25:18-19. Ja. '72. China, birthplace of printing centuries before Gutenberg.

Vital Speeches of the Day. 38:101-2. D. 1, '71. Republic of China; address, October 25, 1971. S. K. Chow.

Vital Speeches of the Day. 38:148-51. D. 15, '71. Fundamentals of the economy; address, November 1, 1971. L. J. Mulkern.

Vogue. 158:156-61. D. '71. China: three photographic insights. Marc Riboud.

Wall Street Journal. p 1+. Je. 30, '71. Calm in Peking: China regains stability, its economy improves, but it faces problems. Robert Keatley.

*Wall Street Journal. p 1+. Jl. 2, '71. Making do: in China, self-reliance is industry watchword—and it seems to work. Robert Keatley.

Wall Street Journal. p 1+. Jl. 19, '71. Getting to China isn't an easy undertaking for non-Presidents; unlike ordinary visitors, Nixon will forgo Tung Fang hotel, dawn music in praise of Mao. Robert Keatley.

Wall Street Journal. p 8. Ag. 11, '71. To understand China, start with Chou. J. M. Roots.

Wall Street Journal. p 24. O. 19, '71. Nixon's trip: what is China seeking. Robert Keatley.

Wall Street Journal. p 1+. N. 2, '71. Made in Peking: goods from Red China begin flowing into U.S.; many are quite costly. Jonathan Kwitny.

Wall Street Journal. p 20. My. 23, '72. What happened to the Chinese. Robert Keatley.

*Washington Post. p C 1+. D. 19, '71. Toil in the farms. Gael Alderson-Smith.

World Politics. 24:182-220. Ja. '72. The dynamics of the Chinese Cultural Revolution. Ching-Do Hah.

World Today. 27:472-8. N. '71. Sino-American relations despite Indochina. J. H. Kalicki.

World Today. 28:14-22. Ja. '72. China's new foreign policy. M. B. Yahuda.

World Today. 28:23-9. Ja. '72. Chinese trade since the cultural revolution. Colina MacDougall.

Yale Review. 61:139-46. O. '71. Biologist's view of China. A. W. Galston.